Easy as
A-B-Z-D

Step by Step Recipes from an Italian kitchen and more

Victoria L LaPaglia

Copyright © 2007 by Victoria L LaPaglia

All rights reserved. No part of this book shall be reproduced or transmitted in any form or by any means, electronic, mechanical, magnetic, photographic including photocopying, recording or by any information storage and retrieval system, without prior written permission of the publisher. No patent liability is assumed with respect to the use of the information contained herein. Although every precaution has been taken in the preparation of this book, the publisher and author assume no responsibility for errors or omissions. Neither is any liability assumed for damages resulting from the use of the information contained herein.

ISBN 0-7414-4356-2

Copy Editor: Michael LaPaglia
Recipe Editor: Carol LaPaglia
Assistant Editor: Camille Conley
Cover Design: Chris Master
Front cover photo by Nicholas Flouton
Back cover photo by Matthew Fillyaw

Questions or comments, email; abzdcookbook@yahoo.com

Published by:

1094 New DeHaven Street, Suite 100
West Conshohocken, PA 19428-2713
Info@buybooksontheweb.com
www.buybooksontheweb.com
Toll-free (877) BUY BOOK
Local Phone (610) 941-9999
Fax (610) 941-9959

Printed in the United States of America
Printed on Recycled Paper
Published December 2007

Introduction

This book started with me updating my Last Will and Testament, and deciding which of my children would get what. It occurred to me that I had many precious recipes that I have collected through the years, some from my grandmother, family and friends. Clearly, I did not want them overlooked and thrown away by accident.

I have a never-ending desire to rid myself of clutter. I am a collector of anything with, "Information I just might need later." I have recipes written on pieces of paper in my junk drawers. My personal recipe book is completely full and ran out of room years ago. I really did need this organization

Cooking has been a part of my life since I was very young when I started "helping out" in the family run Pizza Parlor at about age 8, folding pizza boxes for a penny a box. Then I would turn around and spend the money I just made in the pinball machine.

When I was around 12, my Aunt decided we should all take turns cooking dinner. We would each, on our turn, plan, buy and prepare dinner one night a week. On my night, she would give me $5.00 for the meal and I would spend hours in the grocery store, choosing the perfect foods to prepare that night, making sure to get everything within my budget, including dessert.

After I grew up and moved away to Florida, I loved to make my children's dinner with an emphasis on presentation. Our dinner table was always full of people, and I always made large amounts, so we always had plenty. For me, cooking for my children and an Army of their friends was always a pleasure and a joy.

Our Sunday brunches were legendary in our neighborhood and by the time we moved to the country, we had to set up an extra fold out table to accommodate everyone that came by. This also taught me how to stretch simple ingredients into full course meals.

My daughter is always saying I can make a tasty meal out of anything in the fridge, even if there is nothing in there. I seem to have a gift for this, something I get from Grandma, who could do the same.

The thing about food is sometimes when you eat certain things, the taste sparks a memory. All the recipes in this book were created with some great memories and hopefully when cooking these, new memories will be created and maybe my family and yours can look back on some old memories too and smile.

About baking times: No oven is created equal, and some parts of the country may have air qualities that differ. Most of the baking recipes in this book were created in Florida, low altitude in an electric oven with fresh spring water. Please realize that baking times listed are a guide to cooking. Some may need a little more or less time. Always do a fork or taste test. I noticed when I moved to Georgia, that I needed to adjust my baking time on some of these.

A matter of taste: I love garlic, oregano and mushrooms. I am not a big fan of onions and raisins, so many of my recipes do not include them. You can adjust all of the recipes with what you like. If you like more onions, add them. If you do not like garlic so much, add less. I like to grow my own basil and oregano, so I use dry, powdered and fresh seasonings. Please feel free to add some more of this or change some of that. Your cooking experience should be fun and stress free.

My grandmother did not usually use a measuring cup or spoon and I usually do not use them either, but for this book, I have taken measurement notes for you. The recipes in this book were tested, prepared and approved by my family and friends.

Happy cooking and hopefully this book will help dispel some of the mystery and anxiety you may have had about cooking Italian food. If you have any questions about the recipes or cooking techniques, please feel free to email abzdcookbook@yahoo.com

My Roots

I am the granddaughter of Italian immigrants, Josephine Grippaudo and Felice LaPaglia, both from the area around Enna, Sicily. My Grandfather from the city of Enna, and Grandma from the village of Villarosa. They migrated to America in the 20's where they settled in Brooklyn, NY.

My Great-Grandmother, Vincenza, died during childbirth when Grandma was a little girl. She grew up with her father and nine siblings and told me that when she was little, her father, who was a master furniture builder, would go out every morning and pick fresh fruit from their orchards for breakfast. Everything in Sicily was fresh and organic and nothing came in a can.

When she came to America, it was very difficult for her to get used to the food here. She said here, everything just tasted bad to her and she became very thin, and very homesick. The family here was so worried about her wasting away that her Aunt had to talk sense into her. Finally, after months, she snapped out of it, became the proud woman we all knew and decided her destiny was to accept her fate and stand by her husband here in America. She learned how to adapt her recipes to fit with American ingredients. Still she always made delicious Italian dishes.

They raised four children, Marie, Michael, my mother; Vincenza, and Giacomino. All were born in Brooklyn, NY in the 30's at Kings County Hospital, the same place I was born.

I never had the chance to know my grandfather Felice, but his legacy lives on with fond memories and funny stories about a strong proud Sicilian man who came here to America and lived an honest honorable life working on the docks of New York. His life was cut short one day when he was run over by a drunk driver in 1952 while fishing off a bridge; which was his favorite thing to do. I know that he raised chickens on the rooftop of their tenement building in Brooklyn, sharing with the other families who lived there, fresh eggs and chicken. I also know he would eat a pound of pasta everyday, never gaining an ounce.

I was lucky to be raised by my mother's family and spent much of my childhood living over the family owned Pizza Parlor; Golden Pizza in Kingston, NY. I made my very first pizza when I was eight years old. The local Girl Scout's were touring with us and I was allowed to make pizza with them. I remember my pizza being very round my first time doing it. There was one little girl who's pizza was very strange looking. My uncle said it would be nice if I would give the girl my pizza because hers looked so bad and I could always make another one. I remember agreeing to the switch, but not being too thrilled with the idea, after all, it was my first pizza.

After that, I loved being in the pizza place and worked there with my uncle until I moved away to Florida. I remember while home on visits, I would be happily working behind the counter again, answering the phones and shredding cheese as if I never left.

Going to my Grandmother's in the summer were absolutely my most favorite memories growing up. I was fortunate to get some of Grandma's recipes and take notes while she cooked. She was the kindest women I have ever known and she taught me so much.

Life lessons from Grandma;

*You only have one family and when they are gone, you cannot go around wondering, "What could I have done different".
*You need to be the best person you can be, always, not just when someone is looking.
*Never say anything you're not ashamed to repeat.
*Never be a guest in someone's home and arrive empty handed, be it a host gift or a dinner dish.
*Follow the Ten Commandments in your daily life and you will be a much happier person.

Final note: Italians have contributed much to this country and I am proud to call myself Italian. Some people have forgotten that the United States was discovered (even if by accident), by an Italian, Christoforo Colombo and possibly named for another, Amerigo Vespucci, our roots here go back well over 500 years. Many people don't realize that many of today's traditions, that we all do without thought to where they come from, are Italian born.

I dedicate this book to you Grandma. You were the family rock and the glue that held us all together. Yes, we all had our differences as families do, but you were the constant good between us all.

We can all remember your famous Italian styled extra brown sunnyside eggs, and Shoppa Rite. Your wonderful Christmas treats every year, that you spent weeks preparing. Each one of us getting to eat our favorite. Cuccidata, Struffoli, Sfagliatelle and Sfingi, just to name a few. The care packages that you mailed to us when we grew up and moved too far away to be with you for the holidays. You always remembered what to send each of us.

You were so great and always put everyone before you. Of course, you never felt like you had enough food out when we visited and we always left ten pounds heavier.

We can all remember the strange weed you would pick off the lawn, and turn into an itch relief for bug bites. I still love and use natural healing remedies as an adult.

Grandma, I cannot thank you enough for everything. You were such a remarkable woman. I am proud and happy I had you in my life and we all miss you so much.

Josephine LaPaglia
1909 – 1996

Felice LaPaglia
1898 – 1952

Acknowledgments

Thanks to God for giving me wonderful family who are my friends, and wonderful friends who have become my family.

Thanks to my friends who once upon a time shared with me some great recipes. Even though some of our friendships have come and gone, and we do not keep in touch as we should, every time I make one of your recipes or eat a certain food, it brings me back to fond memories of you and the good times we had.

Thanks to my children, whose appetites have helped create most of these recipes and for putting up with Mom's "experiments" through the years. Camille for the fun we had creating and trying out different recipes. Nicholas for being such a fussy eater when you were little that I had to make alternative solid colored side dishes for dinner every night. "It is a wonder to me that you turned out to be such a great cook yourself." Richard Jr who kept an open mind, great palette and loved everything I cooked, or pretended to, no matter what it was or how it tasted.

Thanks to my brother Matthew, for eating my leftover soup once a week where I literally took everything leftover in the fridge and then turned it into soup. You were sweet never to hurt my feelings and for waiting 25 years to tell me, how bad it was for you.

Thanks to my Uncle Mino and Aunt Charlene for the great family recipes and the old family stories. From that, I know what a forgiving and kind man my grandfather Felice was.

Thanks to my Uncle Mike and Aunt Carol for the recipes, all the advice and helping me so much with history facts and especially for your great editing and final input to help me finish this. Thanks for your recollection of the old days with your dad. I never get tired of hearing about it. I too wish I had known him. I will get to meet him one day.

Table of Contents

APPETIZERS SNACKS AND BEVERAGES	9
BREADS, MUFFINS AND ROLLS	25
SOUPS AND SALADS	39
VEGETABLES AND SIDE DISHES	55
MAIN DISHES AND ENTREES	67
DESSERTS AND SWEETS	105
COOKIES AND CANDIES	135
MISC AND EMERGENCY COOKING TIPS	143

Josephine Grippaudo LaPaglia in 1928 on the Duillo. To pass time, she serenaded the other passengers on the ship all the way over to America. By the time they made it here, she was offered a singing contract with the Metropolitan Opera House in New York singing with the Enrico Caruso troupe. Being married to a Sicilian and loyal to her vows, she politely turned them down. My Grandfather would only allow her to sing for family at parties. My favorite song has always been "Ave Maria", which is one of the songs she sang.

APPETIZERS
ANTIPASTO

SNACKS

AND

BEVERAGES

Steamed Artichoke

This was one of my favorite appetizers growing up. I brought my kids up eating this, and they still love it when I make it. We all gather around a platter and pluck, dip and scrape until the entire artichoke is gone. This will bring the family together at meal times and it is so much fun to eat.

4 large artichokes
½ cup butter
½ tsp garlic powder
1 tsp salt

Cut the stems off the artichoke so they can stand up alone. Peel off any bruised outer leaves. In a large pot put 2-3 cups water (about 2 inches high) and 1 tbsp salt, place the artichokes in, stem on the bottom, cover pot and bring to a boil, then lower to medium and cook for 45-60 minutes. Check occasionally to be sure the water has not evaporated and add more if needed. Test the leaves to see if they are tender enough by pulling out a leaf. It should practically fall off. Do a scrape test. Melt butter and garlic powder for dipping sauce.

To eat an artichoke either everyone gets their own dish or you can place them on a platter with butter sauce in the middle. Pull off a leaf holding only the top, dip the bottom lighter green area into your sauce. Scrape the leaf slightly between your front teeth to remove the soft pulpy goodness near the bottom of the leaf. The rest of that leaf is discarded and you pick another. As you get near the center, the leaves become even more tender and you will be discarding very little leaf. Be careful when you get near the center. There is a part in the middle called a choke. It is a fuzzy prickly thing and completely inedible. Scrape it off, sometimes it just pops off the artichoke heart, but make sure you get it all and discard. Finally, the prize of the artichoke is revealed. The heart is completely edible and the best part. Cut it up and dip the pieces in the sauce. You can also save the heart and use it in the next recipe.

Artichoke Dip

2 large cans artichoke hearts chopped up
½ cup mayo
½ cup ranch dressing
1 cup grated parmesan or Romano cheese
¼ tsp garlic and pepper

Mix well and serve with veggies, toasted French bread or crackers.

If you want to serve this warm, bake for 20 minutes on 350

TIP: Cheese has lots of salty flavor so you do not need to add salt unless you really want to.

HINT: To give this dish a kick add a few drops of Tabasco

Italian Herbed Cucumber Canapé

3 cucumbers
1 8 oz cream cheese
½ cup ranch dressing
¼ cup celery
1 tbsp fresh finely chopped parsley and basil
1 tsp garlic powder and oregano
1 tbsp Romano cheese

Take a fork and score the sides of your unpeeled cucumber. Slice them in 1 ½ inch pieces and lay on their sides. Take a melon baller and scoop out the center of each piece making sure not to go all the way through, turning the cucumber into a little boat.

Dice your celery and cucumber centers together and mix all remaining ingredients together in a bowl then place into a large baggy. Snip off the end of one corner of your filled baggy about ½ inch. Squeeze baggy and fill each cucumber leaving a peak on top. Take some paprika in your palm and sprinkle with your fingers a little on top of each canapé.

HINT: You can also add cooked salmon or crab meat.

Deviled Eggs

This one is a favorite of my son-in-law Charles, who could eat these every day. We have actually added this to our Thanksgiving menu to include everyone's favorite side dish.

6 eggs
½ tsp salt
2 tbsp mayonnaise
½ tsp pepper
½ tsp paprika
1 tbsp relish

In a pot of warm water, place 6 whole eggs in shell with salt, then bring to a boil. Now start timing or start timer for 8 minutes, no longer.

Drain eggs and place them in ice water, drain again and put lid on top of pot with eggs inside and shake pot with a back and forth motion for 30 seconds. This will crack all your eggs and make peeling easier.

Under cold water, peel eggs. Rinse to get off any excess shell then cut your eggs in half and pop out the yolk into a bowl, place eggs on flat plate.

Take a fork and fluff up all the yolks, mix in mayo, relish and pepper. Take a tsp of yolk mix and over fill your egg whites. Put some paprika into the palm of your clean hand, pinch a little to sprinkle on each finished egg. Put into fridge until ready to serve

HINT: The eggs absorb the salt from the water, so beware when adding more salt.

TIP: If you place your hard-boiled eggs in ice water to cool quickly, immediately after they are cooked, this releases a lot of the sulfur, which causes the green ring in the yolk.

Eggplant Appetizer
Caponata

This is one of Mino's favorite treats. Grandma made this for him on her visits to his house in the summer. I do not have her recipe but this is in honor of her memory.

1 large eggplant (boy) see Eggplant Parmesan recipe
2 stalks celery chopped
1 small onion diced
1 sm can tomato paste
¼ cup sugar
1 cup good quality red wine vinegar
2 tbsp capers
½ cup Spanish olives with pimento sliced
1 cup extra virgin olive oil
1 tsp salt
1 tsp pepper

Wash and dice eggplant, place them into a colander in the sink, cover and weigh down for 1 hour to release bitter juices. Cut up and dice all vegetables.

In a frying pan, add ½ cup oil and eggplant and fry until all is tender and golden brown about 10 minutes. Remove them and place onto paper towel to drain. Using same oil add your sliced celery and cook until they are golden brown, take out and drain as well.

In a separate pan add ½ cup oil and cook onions until they become tender and translucent. Add tomato paste and using the same can fill with water and add to pan, add 1 tsp salt, then cook on medium for 15 minutes. Add all remaining ingredients including eggplant and celery, simmer 10 minutes. Let cool completely

Cheese Herbed Bread
Focaccia

Preheat oven to 425

1 loaf uncooked bread dough
(see bread section for recipe, buy frozen and thaw or use 2 canned)
1 tbsp basil or 3 tbsp fresh basil
1 tbsp garlic powder or 3 cloves chopped
¼ cup parmesan
¼ cup olive oil

Roll dough out flat like a pizza. Make finger press indentation all over it. With a basting brush, spread oil all over dough, next sprinkle cheese, then basil and garlic. Bake 12 – 15 minutes. Cut into squares.

HINT: In your grocery's refrigerator department, you can find great loaves of uncooked bread dough ready for use.

Garlic Bread

Preheat oven to 350

1 loaf fresh cooked French bread
1 tbsp oregano
¼ cup softened butter
2 tbsp garlic powder or 6 cloves garlic

If using fresh garlic, put on a small flat pan and roast on 425 for 15 minutes.

Cut your bread in half, lengthwise and spread butter all over both halves. Sprinkle garlic all over, then sprinkle oregano. Bake 15 minutes until you see bread toasting. Slice into 2 inch pieces.

HINT: If using fresh roasted garlic, you need to mix it into butter before spreading.

Pigs in a Blanket

This is a classic and all kids love it. Your children will appreciate this treat.

Preheat oven to 425

2 cans dough biscuits
1 cup shredded cheddar cheese
1 package hot dogs

Cut all dogs in half giving you 20 even pieces.

Open your dough cans and separate. Take one, flatten and stretch it, then put a little cheese on it and place your dog on top with the ends hanging outside the dough, wrap dough around hotdog and pinch closed. Place seams side down onto a greased baking pan. Repeat process until all 20 pigs are done. Bake for 10 minutes.

TIP: You can also sprinkle a little extra cheese on top before baking. Also, you can add 1 tbsp of your favorite hot dog chili inside with the cheese and make chili pigs in a blanket.

Fiesta Cheddar Dip

2 lb Velveeta or cheddar cheese
2 lb ground beef
1 tsp garlic, pepper and salt
1 cup chopped mushrooms
1 large jar medium salsa
1 cup heavy cream
1 bag tortillas

In a pan on medium, cook ground beef with seasonings and mushrooms. Drain excess oil.

In a slow cooker add cheese, meat, salsa, and set on high for 30 minute, add heavy cream and mix, turn slow cooker on low to keep warm. Put your tortillas in a separate bowl.

Stuffed Mushrooms

Preheat oven to 375

2 cups button mushrooms
¼ cup melted butter
1 tbsp garlic powder
1/3 cup breadcrumbs
½ tsp salt
1 tsp oregano
½ tsp pepper
3 tbsp parmesan cheese
Olive oil

Clean your mushrooms and cut out the bottoms, then place them onto a greased baking pan.

Mince the excess mushroom bottoms up and mix with all other ingredients and put 1 tsp bread mix into mushroom caps. Drizzle a little olive oil on top. Bake 10-15 minute

TIP: Add crab meat to the stuffing. This is really good if you are using any kind of crab. I don't recommend using canned crab.

Fried Mozzarella Sticks

1 lb mozzarella cheese block
3 eggs beaten
¼ cup flour
1 cup Italian bread crumbs
1 tsp garlic powder
Oil for frying
1 cup marinara sauce for dipping

Heat your fry daddy or in a large frying pan heat 1 cup of oil

Place in 3 separate bowls flour with garlic, eggs, and breadcrumbs.

You need to cut your block of cheese up into 3 ½ inch pieces. Each about the size of your index finger. Roll to coat cheese into the flour first, then into eggs, and then roll into breadcrumbs.

Place a few at a time into oil and turn after a minute or when you see them turning golden brown. Cook about 2 minutes. Take out and drain on paper towel. Serve immediately with marinara on the side.

HINT: This works with any kind of stringy cheese.

Egg In A Hole

Grandma made this for everyone and we all had this as children. Great for a fun breakfast or a snack.

1 egg
1 slice bread
1 tbsp butter

Cut the center of your bread out (square). In a small frying pan on medium, add butter and your 2 pieces of bread side by side. Crack the egg into the open bread slice and fry about 90 seconds. Then turn over both pieces of bread and fry another minute until egg is cooked and bread is toasty.

Pizza Bread

Preheat oven to 375

1 Loaf Italian or French Bread
2 cups marinara or spaghetti sauce
1 lb sliced or shredded mozzarella
Romano cheese
1 tsp garlic
1 tsp oregano
½ tsp pepper

Slice your bread lengthwise down the middle so you have two long pieces.

Pour sauce in a bowl and mix in garlic, oregano and pepper. Take a spoon and spread the sauce generously onto bread. Spread mozzarella cheese all over the top and sprinkle some Romano next.

HINT: You can add any kind of precooked toppings to this, pepperoni, mushrooms, sausage, hamburger, onion, peppers, olives, spinach, chicken, anchovy.

A friend with Grandma (floral dress)

Cheesy Quesadillas

4 Flour Tortillas
1 cup shredded cheddar cheese
1 small can chopped mushrooms
1 small tomato chopped

Divide your mushrooms and tomato into 4 parts.

Take your tortilla and sprinkle ¼ cup cheese and ¼ part tomato and mushroom onto one side, fold in half and press slightly to level tortilla.

In a large frying pan on medium heat place your tortilla and cook for 3 minutes, then turn over and cook another 2 minutes. Take off and slice in half.

HINT: Quesadilla can be made with many different ingredients including meat on top of your cheese, just make sure you precook the meat before adding it.

Summer Stuffed Tomatoes

4 large tomatoes
1 cucumber peeled and diced (1 cup)
1 stalk celery diced
¼ cup shredded carrots
1 can tuna or chicken drained
2 tbsp hazelnuts or nut of choice
½ tsp pepper and garlic powder
1 tbsp Romano cheese
¼ cup ranch dressing

Cut your tomatoes in half from top to bottom. Take a spoon and scoop out seeds. You can use the inside for the stuffing if you like tomato seeds. (I do not so I toss it.) Mix all remaining ingredients together and over-stuff each tomato, then sprinkle top with Romano cheese. Serve

TIP: You can also use salad shrimp instead of chicken

Party Shrimp Cocktail

This is a party pleaser. Fresh shrimp has that clean summer taste to me. I usually can't buy enough when having company, my kids will eat most of the shrimp before anyone arrives.

2 lbs large shrimp
1 tbsp salt
2 tbsp lemon juice
1 jar cocktail sauce
1 tsp garlic

Fill a pot with warm water, add salt and shrimp and bring to a boil. It takes about 10 minutes. The shrimp should be pink by the time it boils. If not, boil a couple more minutes, and then dump into colander, then place shrimp into an ice bath.

Take your shrimp holding it by the body, feet up and try to grab all the feet at once and pull towards the side of the shrimp, peeling off the feet and the shell usually follows. Peel all the shrimp and leave on the tails. Rinse them off to get all shell debris, sprinkle lemon juice all over, and toss to coat shrimp.

Take a large bowl and fill with ice ½ way. Take a smaller bowl and place it in the center of larger bowl.

Mix garlic into your cocktail sauce, fill the smaller bowl. Then take your shrimp and hang over the larger bowl, letting the shrimp sit on the ice with tails in the air facing out,

TIP: You can also give the shrimp a slight slit where it will hit the rim of the bowl to help it stay in position.

HINT: Your shrimp are perfectly done when pink and not forming a complete circle. If you over cook shrimp, it becomes really chewy and tough.

Sweet Iced Tea

There are many ways to make tea. This is the way I find it easiest.

4 Tea bags
¾ cup sugar
5 cups water

1 lemon quartered and pits removed.

Put 1 cup water and tea bags in the microwave for five minutes or in a pot, bring to boil and simmer for 5 minutes.

In a ½ gallon pitcher, add lemons and drain hot tea water into it leaving tea bags in the cup, add more water to cup, steep and drain into pitcher, fill again with water and steep, then drain for the last time. Add into pitcher, sugar and stir until dissolved add remaining water and fill rest of way with ice. Chill and serve or add ice to glassware and serve.

Lemonade

1 ½ cups lemon juice (6 lemons)
1 cup sugar
5 cups water
1 lemon cut up in slices pits removed for garnish

In a microwave heat up 1 cup water for 2 minutes.

In a ½ gallon pitcher add hot water, sugar, and lemons and mix until sugar is dissolved, add in remaining water and add ice cubes to fill. Place in fridge and chill or to serve immediately, fill glass with ice cubes.

Cranberry Party Punch

I am the punch maker at my daughter Camille's parties. This one is so easy to do. You do not have to add alcohol to any punch recipe, and they will still taste great.

2 bottles Cran-Raspberry juice cocktail
1 bottle Gingerale
2 cups Rum or Vodka (optional)
1 orange
1 lemon

Take your punch bowl and fill ½ ice, add in all liquids. Slice fruit and float on top.

Fruity Party Punch

1 bottle Cranberry juice
1 bottle Gingerale
2 cups orange juice
2 cups Rum or Vodka (optional)
1 large can fruit cocktail

Before the party, take out 4 ice cube trays and fill with 1 tsp fruit cocktail in each department, top with water and freeze at least 2 hours.

Take your punch bowl, add in all liquids. Drop in ice cubes.

> *Sicilian Proverb: Tell me who your friends are and I will tell you who you are. Meaning: A man is judged, by the company he keeps.*

Pretty Party Punch

1 bottle Cran-Strawberry (any light colored juice)
1 bottle Gingerale
2 cups pink lemonade
2 cups vodka or rum
1 pint tri-colored sherbet

In your punch bowl, fill ½ with ice, add in all liquids, then take your ice-cream scooper and float in sherbet.

Fruity Sangria

This is my most favorite wine to drink.

1 large bottle red wine
2 cups Gingerale
1 cup orange juice
1 orange sliced
1 jar maraschino cherries
1 can pineapple chunks

In your punch bowl, add in all liquids, and then add the fruit. Let this sit for 1 hour. Then fill with ice when party starts.

Almost V-8 Spicy Tomato Juice

½ cup tomato sauce
½ cup water
½ tsp pepper
¼ tsp salt
½ tsp Tabasco

In a large glass mix in all ingredients, then pour into an ice-filled glass and enjoy.

TIP: To turn this into a Bloody Mary, add Vodka

This was taken in 1954, when my Grandma (top center) and my mother (sitting next to her) went over to Italy to visit Grandma's family and discuss medical issues.

BREADS
PANE

MUFFINS

AND

ROLLS

Yogurt Banana Bread

Preheat oven to 350

2 ½ cups flour
1 cup mashed banana
¾ cup sugar
2 eggs
1 tsp vanilla
¾ cup yogurt
½ cup butter
½ tsp baking soda
1 ½ tsp baking powder
½ tsp salt

Mix all ingredients, do not over mix. Pour into a greased and floured bread pan.
Cook 60 – 70 minutes, pass fork test

Banana Nut Bread

Preheat oven to 350

2 cups flour
3 mashed bananas
1 cup sugar
2 eggs
1 tsp vanilla
¼ cup water
½ cup butter
1 tsp baking powder
½ tsp salt
1 cup chopped walnuts

Mix all ingredients, do not over mix. Put in a greased and floured bread pan. Bake 60 – 70 minutes

Buttermilk Biscuits

Preheat oven to 425

2 cups flour
2 ½ tsp baking powder
½ tsp baking soda
2 tbsp sugar
1 tsp salt
¼ cup butter softened
1 cup buttermilk

Sift dry ingredients together, squeeze in butter until flour crumbles, and add milk mixing until dough forms. Put on flat surface and knead until dough is smooth. With a rolling pin, roll out to ½ inch thickness and cut with a floured knife cut into 2 – 3 inch strips, then squares or if you have a shape use that. Then place onto a greased flat pan leaving a space between for rising. Bake 15 minutes or until golden.

Charlene's Yorkshire Pudding

This is great to serve when cooking any roast dish. I remember eating this many times growing up as a child and enjoyed this more than the meat dish.

Preheat oven to 375

¼ cup pan drippings from meat
1 cup flour
2 cups milk
2 eggs
¼ tsp salt

Whisk all ingredients together while cooking on medium heat for about 15 minutes. Pour into large cake pan and bake 45 minutes

TIP: You can also put into individual cupcake tins making "popovers".

Honey Cornbread

I always make this with honey because cornbread is so dry and I needed to figure a way to make it moist. Honey is a wonderful ingredient. I use it all the time. Thank you bees.

Preheat oven to 350

1 cup cornbread
½ cup flour
2 tsp baking powder
½ tsp salt
¼ cup melted butter
2 beaten eggs
½ cup honey
½ cup milk

Mix all ingredients together and pour into greased 9 in pan. Bake 20-25 minutes until golden brown.

Original Cornbread

Preheat oven to 350

1 ½ cups corn meal
1 ½ cups flour
2 tbsp baking powder
1 tsp salt
¼ cup melted butter
4 eggs
1 cup milk
1 can creamed corn
2 tbsp sugar

Mix all ingredients together and pour into a buttered and floured baking pan, bake 35-40 min or until golden

Homemade Italian Bread

The trick to bread I have found, is making sure you knead it enough and also letting it rest long enough to do it's combining magic. You need patience when making this. I usually pace back and forth waiting for it to rise enough for the next step.

Preheat oven to 400.

2 cups warm water (not tap)
1 tbsp yeast
1 tbsp sugar
2 tsp salt
5 ½ to 6 cups flour
2 tbsp bread crumbs
Oil to brush on top
Grated parmesan cheese

Put yeast into 2 cups very hot to touch water and let sit for 10 minutes to proof. Add sugar, salt and flour, and knead about 8-10 minutes. Let rise in a covered bowl for 2 hours and punch down, knead again, shape into long oval about 2 in high. Put bread crumbs on cookie sheet, place bread on top, cover, and let rise ¾ hour. Bake 30-40 minutes until golden brown.

HINT: If you have city water, use bottled water instead for better rising results.

TIP: Tap the bottom of the bread; if it sounds hollow, the bread is done throughout.

HINT: My brother Matthew gave me the bread crumb idea instead of corn meal on the baking pan. I love it this way.

Italian Easter Baskets

We made these every Easter growing up with my Aunt Mary. It is a fun and great way to spend time with your kids. I will give you the makings of a small batch, but we made hundred's on Easter and passed them around the neighborhood. I have never come across anyone else who makes this. I hope when you do try it, that you enjoy it as much as I have.

5 hard-boiled colored eggs
1 package flaky Pillsbury dough (10 pack)
multi colored sprinkles
Melted butter for basting

Color your hard boiled eggs with a mix of 1 cup water, 1 tbsp vinegar and 5 drops of blue food coloring or what ever color you like. Let sit in water for around 15 minutes, and then put on paper towel to dry.

Preheat oven to 400 (lower than recommended on packaging)

Remove dough from package and separate all 10 pieces. Flour your hands if needed. Take 1 piece of dough, place a colored egg on its side, in the middle of the dough, and then gently push side of dough up onto the egg about half way. Get a second piece of dough, and split in half. Roll each piece in your hands making a snake shape about 4–5 inches long. Place a strip of dough over your egg from front to back and attach to the bottom dough piece by pinching dough, then do the same with the other half only attach from side to side. You should end up with a cross on the top of your egg making it look like a basket. Place onto a greased baking pan. Do this to all 5 eggs. Brush them with butter and sprinkle on a generous amount of candied sprinkles.

Bake for 10-15 minutes or until golden.

HINT: These are great for breakfast but do not be surprised if they are already gone before morning.

Cranberry Bread

Preheat oven to 325

1 cup flour
¾ cup sugar
2 beaten eggs
½ cup melted butter
1 tsp vanilla
Pinch of salt (1/8 tsp)
½ cup minced cranberries

Mix all ingredients together until combined, adding eggs in last. Spoon into a buttered, floured bread pan.

In a pan of shallow water (water bath), bake for 1 ¼ hours.

HINT: A water bath keeps the air in the oven moist, giving you moist bread.

Pumpkin Bread

Preheat oven to 350

½ cup butter melted
2 eggs
¾ cup sugar
1 tsp vanilla
1 cup flour
1 tsp baking powder
½ tsp salt
½ tsp cinnamon
¼ tsp allspice
1 ½ cup pumpkin (1 lg can) - add last

Cream wet ingredients, mix dry separately, and then blend. Add pumpkin last and mix in.

Pour into greased floured pan.
Bake 50 – 60 minutes, needs to pass fork test

Plain Pancakes

I love pancakes. I can eat them any time of day or night. When I go into pancake mode, I eat them everyday for a week. This is one of my favorite things to have for dinner or a late night snack when it is just me to cook for. My brother, the professed pancake king makes his with peanut butter chips and/or chocolate chips.

2 cups flour
¼ cup sugar
2 tsp baking powder
½ tsp salt
1 tsp cinnamon
1 tbsp vanilla
2 eggs
1 ½ cups milk

Mix together and cook in frying pan on medium to medium low. You need 1 tbsp butter to begin cooking. The pan for some reason does not need more butter. When the pancake has bubbles all over it, time to flip, then they are done about 30-40 seconds later.

TIP: Add ½ cup chopped nuts for crunchy pancakes or you can also do like my brother does, and add ½ cup chocolate chips.

HINT: Use a ladle to make large pancakes and a serving spoon to dose out small ones.

HINT: The first pancake is always the worst looking so this one is for you to taste test.

Blueberry Ricotta Pancakes

I had this while visiting my Uncle Mino in South Carolina. He likes to go online and look up recipes to download and try out. He has files full of recipes ready to make. This is close to one he found and delicious is the only way to describe them.

3 cups flour
2 tsp baking soda
½ tsp salt
½ cup sugar
3 eggs
2 cups milk
1 cup ricotta cheese
½ fresh blueberries

Mix all ingredients, but just until combined, do not overdo.

In a large frying pan or skillet on medium heat, add 1 tsp butter or butter spray. You only need to do this to the first pancake. Use a large serving spoon to dose out your cakes, about 3 onto skillet. When you see bubbles all over the top, it is time to turn your pancake with a spatula. As a rule, the first pancake is usually the worse looking so this one is always for the cook to taste test.

These are great with melted honey all over the top.

Potato Pancakes

This is a wonderful pancake my Aunt Mary used to make. To my disappointment, I have never been able to find any restaurant who serves this. I always end up getting hash browns when I order potato pancakes. Anyway, this is a great way to use up leftover potatoes and it is more of a dinner pancake.

2 cups flour
¼ cup sugar
2 tsp baking powder
½ tsp salt
2 eggs
2 cups milk
2 cups crushed cooked potatoes

Mix all ingredients until combined adding in potatoes last.

In a large frying pan or skillet on medium heat, add 1 tsp butter or butter spray. You only need to do this to the first pancake. Use a large serving spoon to dose out your cakes, about 3 onto skillet. When you see bubbles all over the top, it is time to turn your pancake with a spatula and cook another minute.

I eat this with pancake syrup.

> *Italian Proverb: He, who sleeps in, does not get the fish*
> *Meaning: The early bird catches the worm*

Queen Victoria's Cranberry Scone Bread

Preheat oven to 400

2 ¼ cups flour
½ cup sugar
2 tsp baking powder
1 tsp salt
1 beaten egg
1 stick butter chopped but firm
½ cup milk
¼ cup dried chopped cranberries.
1 beaten egg for egg wash

Mix all ingredients together until combined but do not over mix. It should be very dry, but like a dough and should have chunks of butter throughout. Put into a buttered pan and shape into a flattened oval, brush with egg wash. Score the top down the center then across making four rows. Bake 20 min or until golden brown. Let cool 10 minutes, serve with butter.

TIP: You can add chocolate chips to this instead of cranberries.

Carol's Irish Soda Bread

Preheat oven to 375

4 cups flour
½ cup sugar
1/3 cup baking powder
1 tsp baking soda
1 cup raisins
½ tsp salt
2 cups milk
¼ cup caraway or flax seeds (optional)

Mix all dry ingredients first, then add milk slowly and combine. Pour into a greased and floured bread pan. Bake for 1 hour.

Tuscan Sweet Bread

Here is a recipe straight from Sicily via Grandma.

4 cups flour
1 pkg or 1 tbsp yeast
1 ½ cups warm spring water
½ cup sugar
2 eggs beaten
1 tsp vanilla
½ cup melted butter
½ tsp baking soda
½ tsp salt
Confectionary sugar for icing

Put yeast and hot water in a bowl and let proof for 10 minutes. Sift flour and baking powder into a different bowl and make a well in the middle. Add yeast water and knead until dough becomes elastic and releases from the sides. If dough seems to dry, add 1 tbsp at a time of water. Cover the bowl with cloth & let rise 1 hour.

Punch dough down and work in the eggs first, then salt, vanilla and sugar next. The dough will become very soft, knead for 10 more minutes until it regains the elastic texture again. Now work in the melted butter until all butter is accepted into dough.

Grease 2 pans (8X12) and divide dough into 2 pieces. Press each piece into the pan completely covering the bottom. Now cover with a moist towel and let sit for 1 hour to rise again about double in size.

Preheat your oven to 400 and bake for 25 minutes until golden brown. Take out and turn onto a cooling rack to get the waffle rack design on the bottom as it cools. It will also collapse as it cools.

Flip it upside down after cooling and sprinkle with a heavy dose of confectionary sugar.

Cinnamon Bagels

1 ½ cups hot water
1 pkg yeast
3 tbsp honey
4 ½ cups flour
½ tsp salt
1 tbsp cinnamon
1 tbsp sugar
1 egg

In a large bowl, Mix water, 2 tbsp honey, and yeast and let sit for 15 minutes until you start to see bubbles.

Sift together flour, salt, cinnamon and sugar and slowly mix into water mixture. Knead dough for 6 minutes. Place into a greased bowl, cover and let sit 1 hour.

Take your risen dough and punch down, then cut into 8 equal pieces. Form each piece into a round flat ball, poke a hole in the center and shape into rings. Let them sit for 5 minutes.

Meanwhile preheat your oven to 400, fill a large pot with water and 1 tbsp honey and bring to a running boil. Now only doing a few at a time, drop dough into boiling water and cook 2 ½ minutes, turn over in water and cook other side 2 ½ minutes. Take out with slotted spoon and put aside to drain a little before placing onto a greased baking pan. When you have boiled all 8 bagels, take a beaten egg and brush the top of each bagel. Bake 25 minutes or until bagels are nice and brown.

TIP: Use bottled water for the dough mix if you have city water in your tap. Chlorinated water is an anti-fungal, it will kill your yeast, and your dough will not rise.

We always went to the beach in the Summer.
This is my all time favorite photo of my
mother Vinnie with my Uncles Mike and Mino
when they were young and having fun at the beach.

SOUPS
ZUPPA

AND

SALADS

Fat Burning Cabbage Soup

I discovered this years ago, on my never-ending quest to lose weight. I love cabbage in every shape and form, so this was a no brainer for me to want to make. I have reworked this recipe to my taste. You are supposed to eat as much of this as you like for 1 week. This only makes a few days worth for me.

1 large head of cabbage chopped
1 4 oz can of tomato sauce
6 cups water
1 small onion diced
1 lb carrots sliced or 2 cans
2 cans green beans sliced
1 pkg onion soup mix
1 tbsp oregano
1 tbsp garlic powder or 3 cloves chopped
Salt and pepper to taste

In a large pot, bring all ingredients to a boil, then cover and lower to medium heat for 45 minutes or until carrot and cabbage become tender.

TIP: When you cover the cooking pot, leave it off to the side a little so steam does not build up and cause it to boil over. In addition, when you take off the lid, lift it away from you so the steam does not hit you in the face.

HINT: The cabbage takes a lot of space up in the pot when it is raw. It will shrink down a lot as it cooks.

Chicken Noodle Soup

This soup has special meaning to me. The last time I made this was when my mother was sick in the hospital. I brought her something to eat everyday because I knew she would be missing home cooked food, and this soup was one of her favorites.

1 medium chicken
6 cups water
1 lb carrots sliced
1 small onion diced
3 cloves garlic minced
2 tsp pepper
1 tbsp salt
¼ cup small uncooked pasta (stars, ditalini)
¼ cup Romano cheese

Cut chicken into sections and cook in a large pot with all ingredients, (except pasta) on medium for 1 hour.

Do not drain water but take chicken out and de-bone, cut into pieces and put back in water, simmer another 30 minutes.

Meanwhile cook pasta with salted water al dente about 5 minutes and set aside.

Turn off heat; add in cheese and pasta, let cool for 10–15 minutes before serving. Salt and pepper to taste if needed.

TIP: Romano and Parmesan cheese are naturally salty so check before adding more salt.

> *Romano and Parmesan are very similar, but different. Parmesan comes from Northern Italy and is stronger tasting. Romano comes from Southern Italy and has a more mild taste to it. Both are hard aged cheeses that release their flavor best when freshly grated.*

New England Clam Chowder

2 cans minced clam with juice
½ cup cooked pork (bacon, ham, sausage)
3 cups milk
½ cup water
1 small onion chopped
2 tbsp oil
1 tsp garlic powder or 4 cloves
1 tsp oregano
4 medium potatoes diced
¼ cup shredded Monterey jack cheese
1 tsp salt and pepper.

In a large pot, cook on medium, oil, pork, onion and garlic. Drain any excess oil off. Add clams in juice, oregano, potatoes and water. Bring to boil on high, then lower to medium, cover pan and cook about 15 minutes or until a potato passes the fork test. Add milk and cook on medium-low about 10-15 minutes. Turn off heat and add cheese, salt & pepper.

HINT: The potato acts as a natural thickening agent to the soup. If you like it very thick, add 1 tbsp flour to the milk and mix well before adding to soup.

> *Sicilian Proverb; The words of an enemy can make you laugh, but the words of your friends can make you cry.*
> *Meaning: Ignore your enemies and listen to your friend's advice.*

Sicilian Meatball Soup

This is also called Italian Wedding Soup. The colors of this finished dish are said to marry well together. This is a simple clean dish and easy to do and how can you go wrong with meatballs.

1 lb ground beef
1 egg
¼ cup parmesan cheese
¼ cup breadcrumbs
4 basil leaves chopped or 1 tsp dry
1 tsp garlic powder
½ tsp salt and pepper
2 tbsp chopped basil leaves
4 cups beef broth
2 cups water
1 cup uncooked egg noodles

Mix ground beef, egg, breadcrumbs, cheese and seasoning all together in a large bowl. With your hands knead for 2 minutes until nice and smooth and can form a ball. Now pinch off a small palm full and roll onto little balls, you can use a small cookie scooper, the amount is about the size of a rounded tbsp or walnut.

In a large pot, add your beef broth and water and bring to a boil. Slowly drop in the meatballs and simmer for 10 minutes, then add in your egg noodles and simmer another 5-8 minutes until your noodles are tender. You can add more grated cheese on top when serving.

> *Sicilian Proverb: A person eating must make a few crumbs*
> *Meaning: You have to break a few eggs to make an Omelet. Practice makes perfect.*

Minestrone Soup

1 can white beans
6 cups water
1 small onion diced
2 celery stalks sliced
1 cup shredded carrots
1 cup sliced mushroom - 8 oz
2 Roma tomatoes seeded and diced
1 tbsp oregano
1 tbsp basil
1 tsp pepper
1 tbsp salt
6 potatoes cubed
1 zucchini cubed
1 cup ditalini
¼ cup grated Romano cheese

Cut up all your vegetables. Place the potatoes and zucchini in bowl and fill with cold water.

In a large pot, add water, beans, onion, celery, carrots, mushrooms, tomatoes and spices. Bring to a boil, lower heat and simmer for 30 minutes.

Add remaining vegetables and cook for 20 more minutes.

In a separate pot cook pasta in salty boiling water for 5 minutes until pasta is cooked, then drain and rinse.

When ready to serve add pasta into soup and sprinkle cheese on top.

TIP: You can also add the pasta to each serving. Cooked pasta has a tendency to expand a lot when submerged in liquids.

Charlene's Easy Onion Soup

3 medium onions
2 tbsp butter or margarine
4 cups beef broth or consume
1 tsp Worcestershire sauce
½ cup cheese (your choice)

Slice the onion, then in a large pot, cook onions and butter over low heat about 30 minutes, add beef broth and Worcestershire, cover and simmer for 15 minutes. Put into bowls to serve and add grated Romano or cheddar or any sliced cheese on top.

TIP: Toasted French bread dips really well into this soup.

Oyster Stew

2 cans oysters in juice
1 lb mushrooms chopped
1 onion diced
4 peeled and diced potatoes
¼ cup butter
1 tsp oregano
1 tsp garlic powder
1 tsp pepper
Salt to taste
1 cup milk
1 cup water

In a large pan, cook oysters with juice, onions and mushrooms on medium bringing to a boil for 5 minutes. Add in butter, seasonings and simmer 10 minutes. Add in potatoes and water and simmer about 10 minutes, then add milk slowly and simmer until you start to see bubbles in stew, about 5 minutes. Take off heat and salt to taste if needed. Let cool 15 minutes. Sprinkle parmesan or Romano on top when serving.

Split Pea Soup

Grandma made this the best I have ever had. I used to make this thick and with chunked carrots, but after having hers, which was thin with shredded carrots, I revised my recipe.

6 cups water
2 beef bouillon cubes
1 pound dried split peas
2 lb chopped ham, left over ham or ham steak
1 onion diced
1 tbsp garlic
1 tbsp oregano
1 lb shredded carrots
8 potatoes
1 tbsp. pepper
2 cups water (optional for later)
Salt to taste

Check peas for brown or black ones to toss out. Then put in a bowl of warm water and let sit for 1 hour (or overnight in the fridge).

In a very large pot, put all ingredients in except potatoes, bring to a boil, turn heat to medium, cover, and cook for 3 hours mixing occasionally.

Meanwhile after 2 ½ hours, peel and cut potatoes into 1 inch pieces, add potatoes in after the 3 hours and cook about 15 minutes. During this time, you can pull out your ham if it still has a bone on it and peel the meat off and cut into chunks, then add back into soup.

Now depending on how you like your soup you, add 2 more cups water if you like it thinner or leave it alone if you like it thick. The peas at this time should have disappeared and become a creamed soup. Let cool for 15 minutes before eating (its hot), and sprinkle Romano cheese on top when serving. Salt to taste.

Italian Sausage Soup
Zuppa Tuscany

My friends and I would go shopping on some weekends, and took turns on who would buy lunch. We seemed to mostly end up here. This is my version of a delicious soup I have had at Olive Garden many times with my friends Debby and Sherry.

1 lb Italian sausage
1 small onion diced
4 potatoes
1 cup heavy cream
2 cups water
1 bouillon cube
1 tsp oregano
2 tbsp parmesan cheese
1 tsp pepper
1 tbsp minced garlic (you can also buy this in a jar at produce)
1 tsp garlic powder

In a baking pan, place your sausage logs and diced onions, bake on 350 for 20 minutes, turning half way through. Let cool 10 minutes and then cut into 1 inch slices

Peel and dice potatoes.

In a large pot, add sausage, onion, and all remaining ingredients except potatoes and heavy cream. Bring to a boil and cook for 15 minutes, next add potatoes and cook for 10 more minutes add heavy cream and cook for 5 more minutes.

Let cool a little before serving with some parmesan cheese on top

Sandy's Vegetable Beef Soup

This is from my daughter-in-law Melissa's mom. We are always asking Melissa to make this. It is so good and usually there is never any leftover for lunch the next day.

1 lb ground chuck
½ can tomato paste
1 can mixed vegetable & liquid
1 can corn
1 cans potatoes sliced
3 cups water
3 beef bouillon cubes
2 tbsp garlic powder
1 tbsp salt and pepper
Grated Romano cheese for topping
Salt and pepper to taste if needed

In a large pot, cook chop meat with garlic, drain excess oil. Add all remaining ingredients. Cook on medium until this comes to a boil, let simmer 20 minutes. When serving, sprinkle on some Romano cheese.

HINT: You can also use 4 medium peeled potatoes; dice them into 1 inch cubes.

Italian: When someone sneezes, you bless them immediately to wish and keep them good health. Grandma always said, "Salud!" giving salutations to the person sneezing for good health. This dates back to the first century.

Dinner Fruit Salad

I had this delicious salad with my friend Debbie at one of her favorite Italian restaurants. This is probably the best salad I ever ate and my all time favorite.

1 head dark leaf lettuce
1 cup strawberries
1 tomato
1 cucumber
1 kiwi
1 cup melon
1 cup cantaloupe
¼ cup vinaigrette
¼ cup balsamic vinegar
½ tsp salt and pepper
1 cup sugar roasted walnuts or almonds
½ cup croutons

Slice and cut all the fruit and veggies into bite-sized pieces.

Take a fork and scrape it down the sides of your cucumber before slicing. Cut head of lettuce into large pieces and toss in vinaigrette and balsamic vinegar. Add in fruits, veggies and seasonings. Before serving add nuts and sprinkle croutons all over the top.

> *True Balsamic Vinegar comes from a town called Modena in Italy. It is a sweet aged vinegar and can also be used on many dessert dishes.*

Macaroni Salad

This dish is requested at most parties I am invited to. It is easy to make and easy to please. Actually, today as I am working on this book, a neighbor just came over and invited us to a BBQ, you can guess what he just asked me to bring.

1 Box any shaped pasta
1 can baby carrots
1 can cut green beans
2 cans tuna or chicken
1 cup ranch dressing
½ cup mayo
¼ cup milk
1 cup shredded cheddar
¼ cup Romano
3 boiled eggs sliced
1 chopped pickle
2 tbsp pickle juice
1 tsp garlic and pepper
salt for seasoning

Boil pasta in salty water.

Now mix all ingredients together, saving a little cheddar to sprinkle on top.

This is great warm or cold.

> *Sicilian Proverb: Who ever waits for time to pass only loses time.*
> *Meaning: Make life happen, don't sit around waiting for life to happen to you.*

Matthew's Party Pasta Salad

2 lbs fusili or spiral pasta
1 large red onion sliced
1 green pepper sliced
1 red pepper sliced
2 cans olives sliced
2 lb broccoli crowns chopped small
1 ½ lb tomatoes chopped
2 bottles Newman's Balsamic Vinaigrette Salad Dressing

Cook pasta in salty water, drain water. Mix in all ingredients.

TIP: This is very pretty if you can find multicolored pasta.

Vickie with baby brother Matthew

Garden Pasta Salad

2 cups chopped broccoli crowns cut into small pieces
1 small red onion diced
1 cup shredded carrots
1 cup shredded white cabbage
1 cup shredded red cabbage
½ cup sliced black olives
¼ cup sliced green olives
1 cup cherry tomatoes
1 tsp salt
1 tbsp garlic
2 cups shredded Colby jack cheese (use a brick and shred yourself)
¼ cup parmesan or Romano cheese
1 cup Italian salad dressing
½ cup milk
¼ cup ranch dressing
1 lb uncooked farfale or bowtie pasta

Cook pasta in salted water until done. Drain excess water but quickly put back in pot. You will get a little bit of pasta water in there, which is good. To the pasta add milk and 1 cup shredded jack and ranch dressing and mix up, then let cool completely mixing occasionally as it cools, to help prevent sticking. This coats and seals the pasta with a cheese flavor.

In a separate bowl, mix all veggies together after chopping them up and add salt, garlic, ½ cup Italian dressing and let sit until pasta is ready, about 20-30 minutes.

Then combine pasta, vegetables, remaining cheeses, and Italian dressing. Serve cold or room temp

HINT: This is a picnic pasta salad, no mayo so it can take the heat outside and not spoil.

Italian Style Potato Salad

8 potatoes pealed and cubed
1 small onion diced
¾ cup oil
¼ cup vinegar
1 tbsp parsley
1 tbsp garlic
1 tsp pepper
¼ cup Romano cheese
Salt to taste

Boil potatoes in water until tender. Meanwhile sauté onions in 2 tbsp oil until tender. Drain potatoes and add remaining oil, seasonings and all other ingredients. Mix well.

HINT: This can be served warm or cold.

TIP: Potatoes absorb and cancel out salt during the cooking process, do not bother to salt water while cooking them.

TIP: Since there is no mayo it will sit out without worry so you can even bring this to a BBQ

> *My summers and even some holidays were spent with Grandma and Uncle Mike. He was a NY city cop, he would be at work during the weekdays, and would come home on the weekends where he always had projects going on. I always looked forward to my visits. Grandma and I would take walks at night where she harvested wild Rhubarb leaves when it was in season. I never got a taste for that. We would walk along the roads in the country after dinner and she would point out and name every plant and weed we passed. We dug a plant up with the roots still attached because Grandma told me the root tasted like carrot juice when you boil it and I could not believe this. Well we went home, boiled it and she was so right. To this day, every time I pass Queen Anne's Lace, I feel the need to point it out to whomever I am with.*

Sweet Italian Salad Dressing

¼ cup honey
¼ cup vinegar
½ cup olive oil
¼ tsp basil
2 tbsp Romano cheese
1 garlic clove chopped
1 tsp mustard
½ tsp salt

In a blender or processor, mix all ingredients except oil. Slowly add in oil while blending for 1 minute.

HINT: If doing this by hand slowly add in oil.

Honey Orange Dressing

¼ cup orange juice
¼ cup honey
1 tbsp mustard
½ tsp salt
½ cup oil

In a bowl or mixer, add in everything with oil going in slowly and last. Blend for 1 minute.

Sicilian Superstition: When you hear a cat sneeze something good will happen

VEGETABLES
CONTORNI

AND

SIDE DISHES

Easy Cheesy Asparagus

This is a tasty side dish. I do not prefer this from a can.

1 lb fresh Asparagus stalks
½ cup shredded cheddar
¼ cup milk
1 tsp salt

First when buying Asparagus, I like to look for the smaller, thinner stalks when they first come into season. The regular ones are okay too if you cannot find them. Take your Asparagus and snap off the bottoms. Cut into 2 inch pieces. Put them in a pan of water and add with salt. Bring to a boil, then lower to medium and cook only about 3 minutes and drain.

In a smaller pot, add cheese and milk, and then cook about 3 minutes.

Toss everything together gently and serve.

Delicious Baked Beans

1 large can baked beans or you can use
Pork and Beans with ¼ cup brown sugar added to it.
1 tsp garlic
½ tsp salt and pepper
½ lb ground beef

In a pan on medium, cook your ground beef and drain excess oil when done. Add in remainder of ingredients and simmer 10 minutes.

TIP: I like to use Bush's Original or Vegetarian Baked Beans for people who cannot eat Pork.

TIP: If you like onions, you can sauté a small onion and add it too.

Charlene's Broccoli Salad

1 head broccoli crowns, cut into small pieces
12 slices bacon cooked crispy (can use turkey bacon)
¼ small red onion, diced
½ cup shredded cheddar cheese
½ cup chopped nuts (optional)
½ cup mayo
½ cup red wine vinegar
1 tsp sugar
Salt and pepper to taste

Cook bacon until very crispy and chop into small pieces. Combine mayo, vinegar, sugar until blended and let sit in fridge for ½ hour to set. In a bowl, combine all other ingredients and mix. When you are ready to serve, mix in your mayo dressing.

Sicilian Fried Cauliflower

1 head cauliflower
12 large pitted olives
1 tsp anchovy paste
½ cup olive oil
1 small onion diced
½ cup red wine
¼ cup grated cheese

This should be done in parts, repeated and stirred very gently.

Cut the cauliflower into florets and dice and slice your vegetables.

In a large frying pan, add a little olive oil, garlic and some of the onions and olives, then place 1/3 of the cauliflower and cook on medium a few minutes. Add the anchovy paste and repeat oil, onion, olives and cauliflower cook a few more minutes, then put all of onion, olive and cauliflower and oil last. Cook for 5 more minutes, then add wine, cover and simmer for 10 – 15 minutes until cauliflower is tender and all the liquid has evaporated. Stir in the cheese gently and pour into a serving dish.

Company Corn Casserole

This is a dish I usually make at Thanksgiving. It is simple to make and everyone just loves it.
Preheat oven to 350

2 cans corn with juice
3 cans creamed corn
½ cup sugar
4 beaten eggs
¼ cup melted butter
2 tbsp flour
½ tsp salt
¼ tsp pepper

Mix all ingredients together and pour into a large greased pan. Bake 1 hour until golden and firm in middle

Cheesy Corn Casserole

Preheat oven to 350

1 can corn with juice
1 can creamed corn
½ stick melted butter
1 package jiffy corn bread mix
1 cup sour cream
½ cup shredded cheddar cheese

Mix all ingredients together except cheddar cheese and pour into a 9 inch greased pan. Bake 15 minutes then sprinkle cheese on top and bake for 5 more minutes.

Homemade Linguine Noodles

This recipe made it into this book as a request of my son Nicholas. When my children were very young we used to do this for dinner some nights and it brings back great memories. We would each make our own pastas. I had a butcher block table and we each had our own pile. This is a fun group activity or if you run out of pasta, an easy emergency fix.

1 cup flour
1 large egg
3 tbsp water
¼ tsp salt

First, have everyone wash their hands and give each person a pile.

Pour flour onto a flat working surface. Mix flour with salt then form a circle and make a well. Crack an egg into the middle, 2 tbsp water, and then slowly start to toss flour and blend into egg. Once this egg in incorporated, if it is seems a little too dry add 1 tbsp more water. Make into a dough ball but should be dry enough not to stick too badly to your hands. Cover and let sit for about 15 minutes.

Now flour the working surface and pat down your dough ball. Take a floured rolling pin and start to roll out the dough. Every pass I turn the dough 90*. Do this until your dough is large and about 18 inch flat. Now start to roll the dough into itself like a cinnamon bun. Take a sharp non serrated knife and flour it, then slice ½ inch sections until all is sliced. Gently open the noodles up and make little bird nests out of them.

Take a pot of salted water and bring to a boil. Drop each nest and cook for about 4-5 minutes.

You can eat this with whatever topping you like…oil, butter or sauce.

HINT: Fresh pasta cooks faster than dried pasta and also has more retained flavor. The salt in the water also adds flavor to the pasta, but you don't need as much salt as you usually do for dried pasta.

Egg Rolls
Lumpia

My friend Sally, who was sweet enough to make me lumpia whenever I asked for it, inspired this. Here is my version.

18 egg roll wrappers
3 cups diced cabbage
1 medium onion diced
2 cups julienne then diced carrots
1 cup green beans – French is best
1 small can bamboo shoots chopped
1 can chicken broth or beef broth
1 cup cooked diced or shredded chicken (1 boneless breast)
5 tbsp soy sauce
1 tsp garlic powder, salt & pepper
2 tbsp oil

In a large pot, cook chicken with onion (or ground beef) with onion in a little oil. Drain excess oil then add remaining ingredients together and cook about 10 minutes, until cabbage is al dente (tender with a bite).

Drain out juice into a bowl, but save it for later.

Turn on your deep fryer

Take an egg roll wrapper and put 2 heaping tbsp cabbage mix on center at 1 inch from bottom, fold in sides then roll from bottom up and over. Put on platter seam on bottom. Do all egg rolls this way.

Drop 2 - 4 at a time into fryer depending on size, and turn over after 2 minutes. Put on plate with paper towel to drain excess oil.

Now take that extra cabbage juice you drained and add 2-3 tbsp soy sauce and 1 tsp corn starch to thicken a little. This makes a great dipping sauce for the egg rolls.

Lumpy Mashed Potatoes

This is an all time favorite in my house and I can never make less than this amount. It is usually the first side dish to go.

5 lb potatoes
1 8oz cream cheese
1 cup milk
1 stick butter
1 tbsp salt
1 tsp pepper

Peel and cut potatoes into about the same size pieces and bring to a boil on medium high for 10-15 minutes, until you can stick a fork into them with ease.

Drain and place back in pot, add in cream cheese, milk, salt, pepper and butter, heat on medium-low and with a potato masher (I use Grandma's), not a mixer, start mashing potatoes until everything is heated up. Taste to see if you need more salt.

HINT: The cheese does not overpower so much and it is nice and creamy but still lumpy.

TIP: Put potatoes in cold water and bring that up to a boil otherwise; your potatoes can turn out too mushy.

TIP: Don't bother to salt the water, as you do for pasta. The potato is what you use if you accidentally over salt any dish. When still raw, it absorbs salt, taking the flavor out of the food. So always salt your potatoes after they are cooked.

Italian Superstition: When you move into a new house, you should bless or purify it. This does two things. Brings good luck to you and your family, and expels any negative energy from prior occupants.

Pineapple Casserole

Preheat oven to 350

9 slices white bread (3 cups)
1 can crushed pineapple
3 beaten eggs
½ tsp salt
½ cup sugar
3 tbsp butter
3 tbsp flour
2 tbsp plain bread crumbs for topping

Cut crust off bread and then cut into cubes. Add all ingredients except flour and topping and mix well. Then add flour and mix, and then pour into a 9-inch baking pan that has been sprayed with cooking spray. Sprinkle bread crumbs all over top of casserole and dot with pats of butter on top. Bake 50-60 minutes until golden brown.

Optional topping: slivered almonds, crushed macadamia or hazelnuts.

> *Italian Superstition: The Italian Horn is a protection charm to ward off evil thoughts sent your way. It is similar to "I'm rubber your glue", except it works both ways. Wards off evil towards you, but if you think evil thoughts towards someone while wearing it, your own bad thoughts will bounce off them and back to you.*

Annie's Sweet Potato Casserole

This one is from a Thanksgiving dinner we shared with my old friends Doug and Annie. She made this incredibly yummy dish and I had to have the recipes. It is simply delicious with some interesting ingredients and just as sweet as Annie is.

Preheat oven to 350

First bowl
3 cups mashed sweet potatoes
½ cup butter
½ cup sugar
½ cup evaporated milk
2 eggs
½ tsp each salt, cinnamon, nutmeg and vanilla

Second bowl
¾ cup corn flakes
½ cup chopped pecans
½ cup light brown sugar
½ cup melted butter

Mix first ingredients until smooth and pour into a greased 9 inch pan. Mix second ingredients together with a fork, then sprinkle all over top of casserole. Bake for 20-25 minutes

> *Sicilian Proverb: Walk with your slippers until you can find your shoes.*
> *Meaning: Make the most of the situation you are in now.*

Grandma's Italian Roasted Potatoes

Grandma came to visit me in Florida and this is one of the side dishes she made. Another very simple dish and there were no leftovers that day.

Preheat oven to 425

6 large potatoes
¼ cup olive oil
2 tbsp oregano
1 tbsp garlic powder
1 tsp salt and pepper

Peel and quarter potatoes, then cut each piece into three.

Combine all the spices in a bowl.

In a large bowl, add potatoes, oil, and toss until everyone is coated, then mix in the spices and turn out onto a baking sheet.

Bake 20 minutes, then take out and flip each potato, bake another 20 minutes until potatoes are golden and fork tender

> *Dandelions are an Italian favorite. Not only can you eat the flowers, you can also eat the leaves. My Uncle Mike would go around as a child, collect all the flowers and leaves he could find, and then to help the family, he would sell them all around their neighborhood. My grandmother called the leaves Chiccoria and would cook it up like greens. You can steep dried leaves and make tea. It is said to have many of medicinal purposes. Dandelions have lots of natural potassium in them.*

Sausage Gravy

This is a Southern gravy used in many dishes here in the south, but it is great poured over hot biscuits. It is so easy to make once you know the secret.

½ lb breakfast sausage
¼ cup flour
2 cups milk
1 tbsp salt
1 tbsp pepper
½ cup water

In a pot on medium, cook your sausage until completely cooked. Take your flour, add ½ cup warm water, and mix with a fork. Now pour this into the cooked sausage and oil, stirring non stop until the flour mix has absorbed all the liquids and becomes pasty, cook another 30 seconds. Add in milk, salt and pepper and slowly bring to a boil mixing occasionally so the milk does not stick on the bottom of the pan. Lower heat and simmer 10 minutes until gravy starts to thicken. Take off heat and let cool 5 minutes.

HINT: This gravy gets thicker as it cools.

Zucchini Agridolci
In sweet and sour sauce

6 large Zucchini
2 tbsp olive oil
2 cloves garlic diced
¼ cup red wine vinegar
¼ cup water
¼ cup hazelnuts
2 tbsp sugar
1 tbsp anchovy paste or 2 chopped anchovy (optional)

Clean and cut Zucchini into strips – julienne. Heat the olive oil and garlic, add zucchini cover and cook for 5 minutes on medium. Add vinegar and water and cook for 10 minutes. Add all remaining ingredients and if not using anchovy add salt to taste.

Scalloped Potatoes

Preheat oven to 375

10 potatoes
¼ cup butter
¼ cup flour
2 cups warm milk
1 tsp salt
1 tsp pepper
1 tsp garlic powder
1 tsp oregano
1 tsp basil or 1 tbsp fresh chopped basil
1 cup shredded cheddar cheese
¼ cup parmesan cheese

First peel and thinly slice potatoes about ¼ inch thick. In a large baggy pour pepper, garlic, oregano, flour, and potatoes. Shake to coat with flour.

In a large greased baking pan, pour potatoes in it and spread out evenly. Melt your butter in the microwave for 20 seconds. Pour warmed milk all over, sprinkle salt, then melted butter, ½ cup cheddar parmesan cheese and last basil leaves on top, then cover with foil making air slits and bake 45 minutes.

Take out, sprinkle last ½ cup of cheddar on top, and bake uncovered for 15 more minutes.

> *Sicilian Proverb: He who sleeps with dogs, wake up with fleas. Meaning: Choose your friends wisely.*

MAIN DISHES
SECONDI PIATTI

AND

ENTREES
PRIMIS

Vickie's ABZD
Baked Ziti

This is my signature dish, Baked Ziti. We were at one of my son-in-laws family gathering in Waycross, GA, and I brought Baked Ziti. Since they are not Italian and quite English and very country, my food was foreign to some of them. One of his grandfathers asked me several times to repeat the name of the dish throughout the day. Finally, he said to me, "I am going to call this ABZD so I can remember it." Since that day, we call it ABZD, and he still asks me if I am bringing it. This is our typical Italian holiday dish.

Preheat oven 350

2 lbs ground beef
1 tbsp garlic powder.
1 tsp basil
1 tbsp oregano
1 tsp salt
½ cup grated Romano cheese
½ cup Italian bread crumbs
½ cup sliced mushrooms
1 small diced onion
2 eggs
1 tsp salt and pepper

1 lb ziti or rigatoni noodles
1 4oz package feta cheese diced or crumbled
1 lb mozzarella cheese brick cubed
½ cup shredded mozzarella for top
2 32oz jar marinara or spaghetti sauce
1 tsp sugar

In a large bowl, mix ground beef, 1 tbsp garlic, salt, basil and oregano, ¼ cup Romano, bread crumbs, mushrooms, onions, and eggs. This is your meatball mix. Fry this meat mixture in a large frying pan like a giant flat meatloaf, turn after 10 minutes, also start to chop up as it cooks. Make sure all the pink is gone from the meat. This makes rough meat chunks. Drain excess oil and add all marinara sauce and mix.

Meanwhile, preboil the pasta in salted boiling water, for about 5 minutes. Al dente. Drain water, and then mix crumbled Feta, ¼ cup Romano and cubed Mozzarella cheese into pasta.

Take a large baking pan and from your meat sauce, skim 1 cup mostly sauce to coat pan bottom. Add 1 cup of meat sauce into pasta and mix up before you pour the pasta into baking pan. Top with 2 cups of the meatball sauce, cover with foil and bake 40 minutes. Take out and top with shredded mozzarella cheese, then bake uncovered for 15 minutes.

Heat the remaining meat sauce. I like to add 1 tsp more garlic and 1 tsp sugar to the sauce. This is the extra sauce needed when serving your Ziti.

TIP: Pasta has very little flavor. You add salt in the water before cooking to flavor the pasta. After it is cooked, the flavor will not get inside the pasta. It absorbs the salt better before cooking. Also, for those who don't know, never add pasta to cold or warm water, it will get very mushy and not very good tasting. I learned this the hard way when I was really young and I never forgot how it felt to mess up spaghetti. Always have water at a rolling boil before adding any pasta.

> *Holiday's were held at Grandma's house, on Christmas we would go to bed early because Santa would not come unless we did. There would not be a single present under that tree. It is an Italian tradition to start Christmas at midnight on Christmas Eve, so at midnight we were awakened and to our surprise Santa had really come in the night and filled the room with presents. They were everywhere. That was when the celebration started. We would open presents, eat and had so much fun. Most Italians are Catholic and not supposed to eat any meat when Lent starts until Christ is born, so after midnight you can eat meat. Grandma would have a feast waiting for us. The whole holiday was mangia, mangia, mangia.*

Party Chicken Wings

This is usually made as part of my Super Bowl menu. I make all kinds of finger food dishes and make a buffet on the coffee table. I don't really watch football; I do like to see the new commercials.

Preheat oven to 350

10 lb chicken wings and drumettes
2 cups melted butter
1 cup hot sauce

Cook Chicken wings for 30 minutes on a large flat pan.

Mix melted butter and hot sauce well divide into 2 cup portions.

After 30 minutes take chicken out of the oven and pour off excess grease, then add 2 cups of the hot sauce mix all over chicken. Turn oven to broil and cook for 15 minutes. Turn chicken over and cook for 15 more minutes.

Remove chicken from pan and place in serving dish, then add remaining hot sauce all over chicken and serve.

HINT: These are also known as Buffalo Wings, which originated in Buffalo, NY

> Sicilian Proverb: To a quick question, give a slow answer.
> Meaning: Think before you speak.

Broccoli and Cheese Hamburger Macaroni

Preheat oven 350

1 lb ground beef
½ onion minced
1 tsp garlic, salt and pepper
2 tbsp flour
2 cups milk
1 tbsp butter
2 cups cheddar cheese
1 cup shredded mozzarella cheese
1 head broccoli
1 lb elbow macaroni
1 tbsp salt
¼ cup Romano cheese

Cook ground beef with onion, garlic, salt and pepper, cook on medium and when all cooked through, drain excess oil.

In a large pot, boil water with 1 tbsp salt. Cut broccoli into pieces. Cook pasta and broccoli together about 8 minutes. Rinse and drain.

Next, start the sauce, in a pan, take 1 tbsp butter and melt, then add flour and cook for about 1 minute. Turn the heat to medium low and add milk. Bring slowly to a slight bubbling, mixing frequently. Turn off heat and add in cheddar cheese and ½ tsp pepper and 1 tsp garlic.

Add in ½ cup mozzarella cheese to pasta and broccoli, finally add Hamburger and pasta to cheese sauce and mix up.

Pour it all into a large baking pan and ½ cup mozzarella all over, and then sprinkle Romano cheese on top. Bake 30 minutes

HINT: You do not want to heat up milk too fast or it can separate and curdle, you do not want that.

Carol's Sausage and Mushroom Lasagna

This recipe from my Aunt is very easy to assemble. You will enjoy making and presenting this impressive dish to your family.

Preheat oven 375

12 Lasagna Noodle (16oz)
1 lb Italian sausage
1 lb sliced mushrooms
1 large chopped onion
3 garlic cloves
1 tsp crushed fennel seed
28 oz pasta sauce
32 oz Ricotta cheese
2 cups shredded mozzarella
½ cup parmesan or Romano cheese
1 egg
2 tbsp fresh parsley

Preboil noodles for 5 minutes and bake sausage for 20 minutes. Reserve 2 tbsp sausage oil for later and thin slice sausage.

In a pan, cook reserved sausage oil with mushroom, onions, garlic and fennel until tender about 10 minutes. Stir in Sausage and sauce.

In a separate bowl mix all ricotta, parmesan and 1 cup of mozzarella cheese with egg and parsley.

At assembly time, get a 9X13 baking dish layer bottom with thin layers of sauce, noodles and cheese. Do this until all ingredients are gone. Top with remaining mozzarella cheese. Cover with foil and bake for 50 minutes. Then take foil off and bake 10 more minutes to a get golden brown top.

Chicken and Rice Alfredo

2 lb boneless chicken breast
1 tsp garlic powder, salt and pepper
2 cups milk
½ cup butter
1 cup Romano cheese
2 cups baby carrots (or 1 small bag)
2 cups rice

Take your chicken and butterfly them. Sprinkle salt, pepper and garlic, then in a large frying pan, put a little olive oil on bottom to coat and fry chicken on medium about 6 minutes each side. Take out to cool a bit. Then chop into about 1 inch square pieces.

Put in the microwave, your bag of fresh baby carrots with a hole cut in the top of the bag and cook for 8 minutes.

Meanwhile take a large pot and fill with water, add 2 tbsp salt and rice while cold, (trust me this works), then bring to a boil, lower heat to medium and cook about 15-20 minutes. Taste the rice before you drain the water to make sure it is cooked enough for you. When done, rinse with warm water to get extra starch out. Put back in pot on medium, add milk, butter, cheese, carrots, chicken. Mix to combine, add salt and pepper to taste or as needed. Pour into a serving dish and eat.

TIP: To Butterfly chicken, take your piece of chicken and very carefully slice though the middle of the 1 inch side going only ¾ of the way. Then open cut side out making the chicken twice the size, and this is called butter flying. Helps chicken to cook evenly.

HINT: You can use precooked canned slice carrots if you want.

TIP: I have also done this in a pinch using a Rotisserie Chicken.

Stuffed Chicken Scaloppini

Scaloppini simply means pounded thin

1 lb chicken breast filets pounded thin
½ cup flour
3 tbsp butter
2 tbsp olive oil
1 tbsp garlic or 3 cloves
1 tsp dried oregano
½ onion diced
1 cup mushrooms chopped
16 basil leaves
½ lb mozzarella cheese
½ cup white wine
2 cups chicken broth
1 small can tomato sauce
1 lb any type pasta cooked
¼ cup Romano cheese

In a frying pan, cook onion and mushrooms with garlic and oregano.

If not using shredded cheese, cut the cheese block into French fry looking pieces.

Pound the chicken breast thin, sprinkle with salt and pepper, add cheese, 2 basil leaves and mushrooms into the middle, roll up and pin with a toothpick to keep it closed. You should have enough cheese to do 8 chicken cutlets.

Dip chicken in a mix of flour and poultry seasoning and fry 2-3 minutes on each side in a little olive oil.

Take chicken out and add wine to pan to deglaze, add all of the remaining mushrooms, all other ingredients together except pasta, and Romano cheese in the pan.

Take toothpicks out of chicken and add to pot, then cook over medium about 15 minutes creating a sauce.

Cook pasta in boiling salted water. Take a cup of pasta water out. Drain, add back pasta water and a little of your sauce into it and mix. (about 2 ladles)

Serve with pasta on bottom and Romano cheese on top.

In Italy, most Italians go for a walk after dinner and usually end their night with gelato. After dinner, my family always enjoyed ice cream. There's my grandfather standing in the doorway and my mother, concentrating on her ice cream.

Corned Beef and Cabbage Stew

This is an American tradition that started in the early 1900's. I make this every year for Saint Patrick's Day. Usually I cook this in a slow cooker all day, but this is my recipe for the stove because not everyone owns a crock pot.

3 pound corned beef brisket
1 large head of cabbage
6 cups water
1 medium onion chopped
1 lb carrots
1 pkg onion Lipton's onion soup mix
1 tbsp oregano
1 tbsp garlic powder or 4 cloves
5 pounds potato cut into 2 inch chunks
Salt and pepper to taste when done

Rinse brisket off to remove peppercorns and brine from bag. Trim off excess fat. Place brisket into a large pot, add water, seasonings and soup mix. Cover with a lid and bring to a boil on high and then lower to medium and cook 1 ½ hours.

Cut up your onion, garlic, carrots and cabbage, add to pot, cook for 1 more hour.

Peel and cut up potatoes. Add them to pot and cook about ½ hour more. Total cooking time is 3 hours. Then let cool about 20 minutes.

TIP: Take corned beef out, scrape off extra fat, cut up into bite size chunks, and add back into stew.

Italian Cabbage & Sausage

This is the very first recipe that Grandma gave me. She made it as a side dish with no sausage; this is my variation, but her recipe.

1 medium head of cabbage
1 4oz can of tomato sauce
1 4 oz can water
1 small onion chopped
1 tbsp oregano
1 tbsp garlic powder or 2 cloves
Salt and pepper to taste
1 lb cooked Italian sausage

Quarter and thinly slice cabbage like spaghetti and add to a large pot. Add onion, seasoning and can of sauce.

Fill empty can with water and add. Cook on high until boil then on medium for 1 hour. Stir occasionally.

Meanwhile, cook Italian sausage in oven on 350 for 20 minutes, turning after 10 minutes. Take out and slice up into 1 inch pieces. Then add to cooking cabbage.

When done, pour into a serving dish. Sprinkle parsley and grated Romano cheese all over top.

> *Italian Superstition: A wet bride is a lucky bride. If it rains on your wedding day, consider this good luck. God has blessed your day.*

Stuffed Cabbage

Preheat 350

1 head cabbage
1 lb ground beef or pork
1 cup rice cooked
1 cup sliced mushrooms
¼ onion diced
3 garlic cloves or 1 tbsp garlic powder
1 ½ cup marinara sauce
1 cup water
1 tsp salt and pepper, oregano
½ cup Romano

Pull off cabbage leaves and in a large pot, boil leaves for 5 minutes then put in cold water bath.

In a pan, cook on medium onions, garlic and mushrooms for 5 minutes then add ground beef and cook until all the pink is gone from the meat. Drain off excess oil then add cooked rice, ½ cup marinara, 2 tbsp Romano and spices.

In a large baking pan, mix in 1 cup water, 1 cup sauce and ¼ cup Romano, then take your cabbage leaf and place in the center some rice mix (about a palm full), then fold sides in, then fold in the bottom and top and place rolled leaf seam side down onto pan. Repeat placing cabbage rolls next to each other until pan is filled up. Sprinkle top with remaining Romano cheese and cover with foil leaving a couple of air holes. Bake 30 minutes.

Grilled Asian Chicken Kabobs

2 boneless chicken breast strips
1/8 cup vegetable oil
¼ cup coconut milk
1 tbsp curry powder
2 tbsp honey
1 tsp cumin powder
2 tsp garlic powder
¼ cup teriyaki or soy sauce

Add all ingredients together and marinade for 1 hour. Thread the chicken onto skewers and grill.

TIP: You can do the same thing with Shrimp, make sure you peel and devein them first.

Quick and Easy Chili

1 lb ground beef
1 small onion chopped
3 plum tomatoes
1 16 oz can kidney beans drained
1 16 oz can water
1 pack chili mix any kind
¼ cup ketchup
1 ½ tsp salt
½ tsp pepper
1 tsp sugar for later
1 tsp Tabasco for later

In a medium pot, cook ground beef and onion and drain off excess grease. Add all other ingredients except sugar and Tabasco. Bring to a boil and cook 20 minutes stir occasionally. Add sugar and only if you want it even hotter add 1 tsp Tabasco. Cook 10 more minutes

Crispy Baked Chicken Thighs

Preheat oven to 375

6 chicken thighs
½ cup Italian bread crumbs
¼ cup parmesan or Romano cheese
1 tsp oregano
1 tsp garlic powder
1 tsp salt
½ tsp pepper
1 egg
1 large baggy
¼ cup milk

Crack egg into a bowl and add milk, seasoning, and mix well. Wash off chicken and place in a baggy with egg mix. Seal baggy with all air out and massage chicken so all is coated with egg.

Mix bread crumbs with cheese and pour into baggy with chicken. Seal again and keep rotating baggy to get all the chicken coated with the breadcrumbs.

Now place the chicken on a greased baking sheet and bake 30 minutes, then take out and turn each piece over and bake another 30 minutes.

HINT: As you can see, I prefer baking over frying on many of my dishes. It is healthier for your heart to do this.

Chicken Cacciatore

In Italy, this is called hunters stew. Originally, what ever was brought home after hunting was made into stew. Now it has adapted and become popularly known as this. This was one of my favorite dishes growing up that my Aunt would make.

1 three pound chicken cut into pieces
1 onion diced
1 lb mushrooms sliced
½ cup white wine
1 cup chicken broth
2 tbsp olive oil
2 tsp salt and pepper
1 tbsp oregano and garlic
2 cups marinara sauce
10 potatoes cut into chunks
1 lb baby carrots
¼ cup Romano
1 lb spaghetti

In a large pan, heat oil on medium high and brown chicken on all sides. Add mushrooms and onions and cook for 5 minutes. Drain any excess oil and add seasonings, then wine to deglaze pan. Add chicken broth, carrots and sauce, and bring to a boil. Simmer covered for about 60 minutes mixing occasionally.

Meanwhile, put on a pot of salted pasta water to make your spaghetti. Peel and cut potatoes into bite sized chunks. Add potatoes into the pot and cook for 30 more minutes. Turn off heat and sprinkle Romano cheese all over top and let sit for about 10-15 minutes. It will burn your lips, if you eat it right away, trust me I know. Serve over pasta and sprinkle Romano cheese on top.

Salvation Chicken Lo Mein

My good friend Sally who is from the Philippines, taught me this dish. This is my slightly modified version. We took turns having each other over for dinner every night since she lived right upstairs from us and we did everything together when our children were little.

1 lb boneless chicken chopped
1 bag rice sticks
1 bag frozen veggie mix- broccoli, carrots and cauliflower
1 cup sliced mushrooms
½ cup soy sauce
¼ cup sweet and sour sauce
1 tsp garlic powder and pepper
Salt to taste

Brown chicken in frying pan, add everything except rice sticks and cook for 15 minutes stirring frequently.

Meanwhile in a pot, bring water and 1 tbsp salt to a boil, add rice sticks and cook 4 minutes, then drain and rinse.

When ready to serve, get a large serving bowl, add all ingredients, and mix together.

Carol's Italian Style Pork Chops

4 Pork Chops
2 tsp sage, garlic powder and rosemary
2 tbsp butter
2 cups water
¼ cup white wine

Mix seasonings and rub onto chops. In a frying pan put 2 tbsp butter, then on medium heat, brown chops on both sides. Add 2 cups water to help deglaze pan, cover pot and cook for 1 hour turning chops occasionally. Add wine and cook for 2 more minutes. Serve with your choice of side dish.

Chicken Whoppers

This is a favorite in our house, and as good as any Burger King. I buy the big sesame buns for this one.

3 large Chicken breasts
Salt, pepper and garlic powder to season chicken
6 sesame buns
Lettuce leaf slices
1 Large tomato
¼ cup ketchup
¼ cup mayonnaise
½ tsp salt and pepper
Sliced onion (optional)

Take your chicken and butterfly them, then cut the chickens in half. Sprinkle salt, pepper and garlic, then in a large frying pan, put a little olive oil on bottom to coat and fry chicken on medium about 5-8 minutes each side. Take out to cool a bit.

Mix ketchup, mayo, salt and pepper in a bowl for special sauce topping

Take your bun and place 2 or 3 lettuce leaves, then chicken, a slice of tomato, on the top of the bun spread a healthy dose of special sauce and top. You now have the perfect chicken whopper.

Italian Proverb: Help yourself and God will help you.
Meaning: God helps those who help themselves.

Cowboy Casserole

This is my version of Shepherds Pie with an Italian twist. Since I use beef instead of lamb I call it this. My kids love this one a lot!

Preheat oven to 350

1 lb ground beef
½ cup sliced mushrooms
1 package Lipton's onion soup mix
½ cup Italian bread crumbs
1 egg
1 tsp garlic powder or 2 cloves
½ tsp Salt and pepper
2 tbsp olive oil
10 potatoes
½ cup milk
4 oz cream cheese (½ of a big one)
1 can corn
1 cup baby carrots (small bag)
1 can cream of mushroom or chicken soup
¼ cup Romano cheese
½ cup shredded cheddar for top.

In a large bowl, mix ground beef, mushrooms, onion soup mix, bread crumbs, egg, and seasonings in a frying pan. In a large frying pan on medium cook for 10 minutes without to much touching, then start to chop and turn over to cook the other side. Make sure all is cooked before you drain excess oil.

Peel and cut up potatoes for boiling. Drain when fork tender then mash and add ½ cup milk, 1 tsp salt, pepper, garlic, and cream cheese.

Microwave the baby carrots in their bag with a hole in it for 8 minutes. Then add to a bowl with corn and 1 can soup.

Assemble in a baking pan Hamburger on the bottom, vegetables in the middle and top with mashed potatoes. Sprinkle Romano and cheddar cheese on top and bake 30 minutes. Serve with gravy.

Manicotti

Preheat oven to 350

1 box manicotti shells
1 lb ricotta cheese
1 egg
1 lb block mozzarella cheese
¼ cup parmesan cheese
3 cups marinara or spaghetti sauce
1 tsp garlic powder
1 tsp oregano
1 tsp salt and pepper

In a pot of salted boiling water, preboil manicotti shells for 4 minutes on medium. Drain and rinse. Meanwhile shred the mozzarella cheese.

In a large bowl, mix Ricotta cheese, egg, seasonings, and 1 cup shredded mozzarella together. If using fresh Ricotta, add ½ cup pasta water. Fresh Ricotta is much drier than the store bought cheese. Put entire mixture into a large baggy and snip a ½ inch or smaller hole into the bottom corner.

In a large baking pan, spread 1 cup marinara. Take your manicotti and squeeze cheese into one side, then squeeze into the other side and fill shell, place on top of sauce in the baking pan. Repeat this filling process until you run out of room or ingredients making only one layer of shells. Spoon remaining sauce all over the top and cover with foil tent, make a few air slits in the foil. Bake 40 minutes. Take out and add 1 cup shredded cheese and parmesan and bake uncovered 20 more minutes. Let cool about 15 minutes.

TIP: For variety, add ½ lb cooked ground beef or ½ cup minced mushrooms to the mix.

Crab Manicotti: you can make this by adding ½ cup lump crab into the cheese mix and instead of using marinara make Alfredo sauce by cooking in a pot, 2 cups milk, 1 cup Romano and ½ cup butter and pour over manicotti.

Mike's Sausage Eggplant Parmesan

This is one of my Uncle's specialties. This fancy dish is so stress free and your family will definitely be impressed. I was happy to see this easy version to what I have been doing for many years and it tastes delicious.

Preheat oven to 350

3 medium eggplants
2 large cans crushed or whole tomatoes
2 garlic cloves diced
1 tsp and oregano, basil, Salt and pepper
1 lb block mozzarella cheese sliced thin
Oil for basting and frying
1 lb Italian Sausage
1 cup Italian breadcrumbs
1 tsp salt, pepper, oregano, basil
2 garlic cloves diced
½ cup parmesan or Romano cheese grated

Take your eggplant and peel, and then slice ½ in thin. Place onto a greased cookie sheet and brush top with oil, broil for about 10 minutes until you see eggplant starting to turn golden brown. Flip over and brush oil on other side the bake another 10 minutes.

Meanwhile, fry sausage links in 2 tbsp oil and let cool. Also, start the marinara sauce by cooking on medium heat, tomatoes, garlic and seasonings until it is reduced, and becomes thick. 20-30 minutes. Slice sausages, then add to cooked sauce after is done.

Next, get your breadcrumb mix ready by mixing breadcrumbs, seasonings, garlic and parmesan cheese together.

At assembly time get a baking dish and put about ½ cup sauce on the bottom to lightly coat pan entirely. Add a layer of eggplant making sure you cover bottom completely, so overlap if you need to or cut shapes to fill in blank spots.

Spoon sauce all over top, and then add sausage throughout, next sprinkle a light coating of bread crumb mix all over.

Add thinly sliced mozzarella cheese. Repeat this until you run out of layering room or eggplant. You want to end with lots of mozzarella cheese on top. Discard excess bread crumb mix. Take foil or lid and completely cover baking dish. Give some air slits for steam. You can also save your top layer of mozzarella cheese and put it on 15 minutes before done. Bake 40 minutes, then let sit for 15 minutes to set before cutting into it.

Italian Superstition: On New Years Eve, take new coins; penny, nickel, dime, quarter, half and whole dollar and place them face up on your window sill before midnight for good luck in the following year.

Eggplant Parmesan

Preheat oven 350

2 large eggplants
3 eggs
1 cup milk
2 cups flour
2 cups Italian breadcrumbs
Salt and pepper
Oil for frying
1 tbsp garlic powder and oregano
2 can tomato sauce
2 lb block mozzarella cheese
½ cup Romano cheese grated

First, make your battering station. One bowl with eggs and milk mixed well. One with flour with ½ tsp each salt & pepper. One with bread crumbs and 2 tbsp Romano cheese mixed into it.

Next step is very messy and feel free to rinse fingers off occasionally during this procedure but dry them well. Take your eggplant and dip both sides into flour, next into the milk bath, then into bread crumbs and put on platter. Do this to all eggplant slices.

You can now cook these 2 ways;

1 - Heat up a large frying pan with about 1 ½ inch olive oil. To check if oil is ready, I wet my fingers with water and splatter into oil making sure to pull back. If this makes little bubbles in oil, you are ready to fry your eggplant. Fry them about 7 minutes on medium and turn cooking another 3-4. Do this until all are fried.

2 - Sometimes I put onto a large cookie sheet and bake them on 350 for 20 minutes. Turning after 15 minutes. Make sure to preheat oven if you choose this method.

Pour sauce into pan or bowl, add 1 tsp salt, pepper, oregano and garlic powder.

At assembly time get a large baking dish, put enough sauce to coat bottom, add a layer of eggplant making sure you cover bottom completely, and overlap if you need to or cut shapes to fill in blank spots. Spoon sauce all over top Add sliced mozzarella cheese and sprinkle Romano all over top. Add more eggplant, sauce, and cheeses and do this until you run out of layering room or eggplant. You want to end with cheese on top. Take foil or lid and completely cover baking dish. Give some air slits for steam. You can also save your top layer of mozzarella cheese and put it on 15 minutes before done. Bake 1 hour, then let sit for 15 minutes.

TIP: If you want less seeds you need to make sure you get an eggplant with a circle on the bottom, this is considered a male. The one with an oval or slit is loaded with seeds and are considered female.

HINT: Cut your eggplant into ½ inch slices. Stack them all into a colander in the sink and cover with a paper towel. Add a heavy pot or object to the top to weight them down for about ½ hour. This helps release some of the bitter juice inside the eggplant you really do not want.

> *In Italy, on Christmas Eve, the children would set out their shoes so Mrs. Claus could fill them with candies and toys. This is La Befana. If they were good, they wake up with their shoes full of treats. If they were bad, they wake up with coal in their shoes. Today we use stockings.*

Baked Lasagna

There may be an easier way to do this special occasion dish, but this is my organized old fashioned way to make it.

Preheat oven 350

1 lb ground beef
2 tbsp garlic powder.
1 tbsp fresh basil
1 tbsp oregano
½ cup sliced mushrooms
¼ medium chopped onion
1 tsp salt and pepper
1 lb Italian sausage
1 lb lasagna noodles
1 lb mozzarella cheese brick sliced thin
1 lb ricotta cheese
1 8 oz cream cheese
1 egg
¼ cup parmesan or Romano cheese
½ cup shredded or sliced mozzarella for top
2 32oz jars marinara or spaghetti sauce

Preboil your pasta in salted water for about 5 minutes. Al dente. Drain water and take parchment paper and place noodles outstretched onto it, place more parchment paper on top and repeat until all noodles are lying flat and stacked. I do this because the noodles stick together like they were glued after they are cooled down, and if you separate them while they are warm, you can take your time assembling the dish.

Now cook your sausage in the oven on 350 for 20 minutes turning half way between. Slice into 1 inch pieces.

Meanwhile, in a large pot on medium, cook ground beef, mushrooms, onions and seasonings for 15 minutes. Drain out excess oil and add in 1 jar marinara sauce and sausage when ready.

Slice your mozzarella and cream cheese. Take your Ricotta cheese and mix in 1 egg, 1 tsp garlic powder and 1 tsp oregano.

Take a baking pan and about 1 cup sauce to bottom. Layer noodles on the bottom of a large thick baking pan overlapping each other. Spoon on ½ the Ricotta mix, and ½ the cream cheese. Spoon on meat sauce, layer on sliced mozzarella, sprinkle Romano, place another layer of noodles, press down slightly with a spatula and repeat but save a little sauce for the topping. Top with noodles, use remaining sauce, and sprinkle shredded or sliced mozzarella cheese and a little Romano on top. Cover with foil tent leaving air holes and bake for 1 hour. Let cool 15 minutes before cutting into it so the cheese has a chance to set up.

HINT: Foil Tent is 2 pieces of foil scrunched together to make a larger piece and tent over dish so the top of the foil does not hit the top of the food. I do this so the cheese does not stick to the foil.

TIP: You can buy shredded cheese if you want, but I recommend the block over shredded. Your cheese will have a much fresher flavor to it if you shred or slice it yourself.

Matthew's Sweet and Sour Meatballs

This one is a crowd pleaser. We always beg my brother to make this. There are always one or two of us sneaking in the pot.

2 lbs ground beef
2 packages onion soup mix
2 tbsp oil
1 12oz jar grape jelly
1 12 oz jar chili sauce
1 cup uncooked rice
1 tbsp salt for rice water

Mix all ground beef and onion soup mix together and form into little 1 inch meatballs. Fry these in oil on medium until done about 10 minutes.

In another pan on medium heat, mix jelly and chili sauce, then add drained meatballs and cook for 20 minutes

Meanwhile, while that is cooking, make your rice.

> *My secret to perfect rice: Take a large pot and fill ¾ up with cold water, add 1 tbsp salt and rice, bring water to a boil, lower to medium and cook 15 – 20 minutes, until rice is done. Taste to make sure it is cooked. Drain and rinse rice like spaghetti. Your rice will never stick like glue when you do this method. You also rid yourself of that extra starch in the rice that would stick to your hips later.*

Italian Style Meatloaf

I made this once with a plain meatloaf for the fussier eaters. This one disappeared first and was eaten by everyone including my picky eaters

Preheat oven to 350

2 pounds ground beef
2 tbsp olive oil
1 green pepper, seeded, small diced
1 onion, diced
1 cup mushrooms sliced
3 cloves chopped garlic
2 eggs
1 cup bread crumbs
1 tbsp any beef sauce – I like Dales, but you can use Worcestershire
1/2 cup grated Romano
1 tbsp basil
1 tbsp oregano
1 teaspoon salt
1 teaspoon black pepper
½ cup spaghetti or marinara sauce
¼ cup grated Romano for top

In a large pan on medium, cook the peppers, onions, mushrooms and garlic for about 5 minutes. Turn off heat and let cool a few minutes. Meanwhile, combine all of the remaining ingredients except the sauce in a large bowl. Now mix in the cooked veggies. Pack the meat mixture into an oiled loaf pan or oval shape it onto a cake pan. Cover with foil leaving an air hole for steam.

Bake for 45 minutes. Take off foil tent, add sauce and extra Romano and cook another 20 minutes. Remove from the oven and let cool for 5 minutes.

TIP: My grandmother used to add ½ cup slivered almonds for extra crunch.

Grilled Mushroom Hamburgers

2 lbs ground beef
1 packages onion soup mix
2 tbsp mayonnaise
½ cup chopped mushrooms
½ cup Romano cheese
1 tsp garlic

Clean your grill off and then spray with cooking spray. Start your charcoals.

Mix all of the ingredients together. Then take a big handful and form the patties, placing them on a platter. Take them to the grill and place gently, do not touch them for 10 minutes, or until you are sure they are done at least half way through the middle. They usually will release from the grill easier the more cooked they are. Flip them over and cook another 5 minutes or so depending on how you like it. Well done will take the longer than medium.

HINT: Your burgers are going to shrink in and plump up, so form them flatter and extra big compared to your bun.

> *I have a large grill frying pan for indoor grilling right on my stove, for me it works great and just as well as an outdoor grill but without the smoke. You get great grill marks and if you are cooking for one or more, weather does not matter. If you do not already have one, invest in one, they are great.*

Camille's Stuffed Peppers

Preheat oven to 350

4 green peppers
1 lb package Spanish yellow rice mix
1 can diced tomatoes
1 clove garlic
½ small onion diced
½ lb ground beef
1 cup shredded cheddar

Cook your yellow rice following directions on the bag.

Meanwhile, in a pot on medium, cook ground beef with onion and garlic and drain excess oil. Mix in tomatoes and cooked yellow rice

Cut the tops off the peppers and save for later. Take your hands, pull out all the seeds, and clean out the inside of the pepper. Rinse to make sure you get all the seeds. Take a spoon and overfill your peppers with rice mix, then place then onto a baking pan. Put the tops back on and bake 30 minutes.

Take your peppers out of the oven and remove tops gently. You will see that your filling has settled and this is where you mound shredded cheddar cheese into the pepper, then place their tops back on and bake for 15 more minutes. Let them cool for 10 minutes and serve

TIP: Another way to make this is to cut your peppers down the center and stuff each side. The only thing you can't do, is give each pepper a cute hat.

Italian Poor Man Stew

This was a main request in our home when I was growing up. I remember having this for dinner at least twice a week and looking forward to it too. It was always called Poor Man Stew. I still make this and sneak it into my no carb diet sometimes. I can't help it, I need it.

1 lb ground beef
½ onion minced
1 tbsp garlic,
1 tbsp oregano
1 tbsp basil
1 tsp pepper
1 jar spaghetti sauce
1 lb pasta, any type, fusili works good
Salt to taste
¼ cup grated Romano cheese
1 tsp sugar

Cook ground beef with onion and spices on medium and when all cooked through drain excess oil and add the sauce, sugar, and cook about 15 minutes on medium to low, then remove from heat.

Meanwhile, in a large pot, boil water with 1 tbsp salt. Add pasta, bring to boil, then lower to medium heat, and cook about 8 minutes. Rinse and drain.

When ready to serve, add pasta and cheese into sauce and mix. Serve with a sprinkle of Romano on top.

> *Sicilian Proverb: Except in the eyes of God, not all men are created equal, so we are all responsible to help those who cannot help themselves.*

Salmon Patties

One day while my mother and I were visiting Mino's, they started reminiscing, she brought up a house they lived in on a canal. The whole neighborhood was built on water. They spoke about the fun they had fishing off their back porch and catching dinner many nights. I know they have salmon up there in NY, but I don't think it swam through their neighborhood.

2 cups salmon
1 egg
1 small onion diced
2 tbsp Romano cheese
2 cloves garlic diced
1 tsp oregano
1 tsp salt
1 tsp pepper
1 cup Italian bread crumbs

Mix all ingredients together and form into 1 inch thick oversized patties. In a flying pan on medium, sprinkle bottom with olive oil and heat 1 minute, add in patties and fry about 5 minutes, check to see if it is brown on the bottom, if so, turn over and cook until other side is golden brown. Place onto buns and serve with choice of condiments.

Quick Tarter Sauce

¼ cup mayonnaise
2 tbsp relish or about half a minced pickle
1 tsp lemon or vinegar
1 tsp Dijon or ground mustard
Pinch of salt

Shrimp Fra Diavolo

1 lb shrimp peeled and deveined
3 tbsp olive oil
2 tbsp garlic
½ tsp crushed red pepper
1 tbsp oregano
½ cup wine
2 cans crushed tomatoes with juice
1 tsp parsley, salt and pepper
1 lb spaghetti cooked

Cook all ingredients except tomatoes and spaghetti on medium until wine reduces by half about 15 minutes, add tomatoes and simmer 5 minutes. Add shrimp and cook 5 more minutes, until shrimp has turned pink. Serve over cooked spaghetti

Shrimp Marsala

1 ½ cups soup stock
½ cup Marsala wine
2 tbsp olive oil
1 cup diced tomatoes in juice
1 cup mushrooms sliced
1 sm onion diced
½ cup sour cream
1 tbsp garlic
1 tsp salt and pepper
2 tbsp flour
½ cup milk
¼ cup parmesan cheese
1 lb shrimp peeled and clean
1 lb spaghetti cooked

Cook mushrooms and onions medium in a large pan for 15 minutes. Now sprinkle flour on and cook about 2 minutes. Add soup stock, wine, tomatoes and seasonings and bring to boil then simmer 5 minutes. Add milk and bring to slow boil. Add shrimp and cook 5 more minutes. Mix into cooked pasta and add grated cheese on top.

Melissa's Famous Tater Tot Casserole

Preheat oven to 350

1 ½ lbs ground beef
1 tsp garlic powder
1 tsp oregano
1 tsp Salt and pepper
1 large can cream of mushroom soup
1 bag frozen tater tots
2 cups shredded cheddar cheese

In a frying pan on medium, cook and brown ground beef with seasonings, then drain out excess oil.

In a large baking pan, pour in cooked ground beef, top it with the cream of mushroom soup, and spread evenly. Now layer on ½ a bag of tater tots and 1 cup cheese, then ½ bag tater tots and remaining cheese.

Bake for 30 minutes and make sure cheese is melted and tots are nice and hot.

> *Marsala Wine is a fortified, aged wine that only comes from Sicily. It has a rich smoky flavor and varies from sweet to dry in taste. It comes in 3 colors and is used to enhance many dishes including dessert.*

Spaghetti and Meatballs

This is my favorite meatball recipe and is used in many of my dishes. I remember my Aunt Mary telling me how embarrassed she was when the family went to the beach in the Summer as children. During lunch, they would crank up the old barbecue and bring out the pots to fill with water and boil spaghetti, because they ate spaghetti everyday no matter what was going on.

1 lb ground beef
1 lb ground pork
1/4 cup Romano or parmesan cheese
1 cup bread Italian crumbs
1 small onion minced
2 eggs
¼ cup chopped mushrooms
1 tbsp garlic powder or 2 cloves
1 tsp basil and oregano
1 tsp Salt and pepper

1 32 oz jar Marinara sauce
1 lb spaghetti

Mix all ingredients together in a bowl, except sauce and pasta. Form your meatballs. Palm size is my preference but you can go bigger. Roll in flour to coat lightly.

In a frying pan put a little olive oil and cook on medium. They are ready to turn when the meat releases from the pan, or in a 325 oven, place all meatballs on a greased flat pan and cook for 20 minutes, then turn them over and cook for 10 more.

In a pot add sauce and meatballs and simmer for 15 minutes. I like to add 1 tsp more garlic and oregano and a tbsp sugar if using a store bought sauce.

Boil pasta last in salted water and drain. Sprinkle Romano cheese over top of dish when assembled for extra flavor.

TIP: No breadcrumbs, takes 4 slices of bread, tear into pieces and soak in ½ cup milk, squeeze most of the milk out but not too tight or your bread will solidify. Break into little pieces and add to meat or you can also use ½ cup oatmeal instead of breadcrumbs.

TIP: My grandmother would roll the formed uncooked meatballs into flour before frying, to help seal in the flavor and make meatballs crunchier on the outside

HISTORY OF SICILY AND ITS PASTA

The Greeks were one of the first to rule Sicily around 800 BC. It did not actually become part of Italy until World War 1; after Garibaldi freed them from Spain.

Pasta was first introduced to Sicily by the Arabs, who ruled that country for about 200 years during the eighth century. According to historians, pasta originated with the Arabs.

The Chinese were actually one of the first to dry pasta out, which resulted in it being stored and shipped to other countries but that was not until the 13th century.

Turkey with Italian Style Stuffing

Being an American holiday, Italians coming to this country did not celebrate Thanksgiving. When they embraced being American, they adapted the holiday to include their Italian dishes. When I was young, we always did Thanksgiving at my Grandmothers and our dinners always start with an Italian dish as the appetizer. After growing up and moving to Florida, my friends and family would all take turns on whose house would host the dinner. Who ever the guest was, they would usually bring the Italian dish.

1 Whole Turkey
Bag and neck from inside Turkey
1 ½ cups butter melted
1 tsp salt
1 large bag stuffing mix – crouton style
2 medium eggs
1 small onion chopped
1 cup mushrooms chopped
1 lb ground chuck
1 lb Italian sausage
½ cup slivered almonds
1 cup chicken broth
1 cup water
1 tbsp oregano, garlic powder, basil
2 bags mixed vegetables
Salt and pepper to taste

Three days before, take Turkey out of the freezer and move to fridge or buy your turkey.

Night before, either rub ½ cup melted butter and 1 tsp salt all over turkey, seal with aluminum foil, and put into fridge.
Or night before get a turkey injector and inject all throughout turkey, melted butter or basting mix.

Night before empty turkey parts from inside, both sides of turkey and cook in 4 cups of water, including the neck on medium, cover and cook about ½ hour. Let this cool, and then put it in fridge for the next day, water broth included.

Night before peel skin off sausage, and cook with ground chuck, mushrooms and onion and seasoning. Drain off excess oil and let cool, then refrigerate.

TIP: The night before, figure how long your turkey will cook, and what time you would like to serve it. Use the following formula: cooking on 350 for 15 minutes per pound if not stuffed. 20 minutes per pound if stuffed. That would be 4 pounds per hour unstuffed and 3 pounds per hour stuffed. Then when you decide how long it will take to cook, deduct that time from your serve time and deduct 30 minutes for prep time. That is the time you need to start the turkey the next day.

On Turkey day

In a very large pan put all your cooked meat and mushrooms, stuffing mix, eggs, almonds, cup of melted butter, chicken broth. Cut up into little pieces, your turkey ingredients cooked from the night prior. Gizzards have very tough exterior so I usually cut the hard parts off and give it to my dogs. The turkey neck will give you a little meat but most of that will get tossed. Add what you cut up into the stuffing mix. Mix thoroughly, should be a very wet oatmeal feel. If not add a little more water. Add about 1 tbsp pepper and salt.

This will stuff around a 20 lb turkey. I do this with my hands to get the stuffing in deep. Pour all around bottom of your turkey pan both bags of vegetables. The stuffing you have left after filling your bird can be put in a covered pan and placed in the oven for 1 hour before turkey is done. Bake on 350.

If you don't have a pan cover, make a foil hat for it by taking 2 long pieces of foil and rolling them together to make a square shape to cover your turkey. Do not forget air slits in the foil. This helps by basting your turkey. Also, if you want your turkey skin crispy take the foil off ½ before cook time is up. Then when done let the turkey sit for about ½ hour. This will ensure each piece of your turkey stays juicy.

Lori's Western Stew

Lori is one of my oldest friends from New York who now lives in Florida. This is one of her favorite dishes that her mom made for her as a child, she was nice enough to share it. This is so delicious and so easy to make.

Preheat oven to 350

2 lbs stew beef
1 lb baby carrots
1 medium onion diced
6 large potatoes
1 16oz bottle Catalina Salad Dressing
1 10 pack can refrigerator biscuits for later
Pepper to taste

Marinate the beef in ¼ cup of the Catalina for 2 hours or overnight.

In a large frying pan on medium heat, brown your onion and stew meat on all sides. Place into a baking pan with remaining Catalina and cover with foil, bake for 1 hour.

Meanwhile peel and cut up potatoes into bite sized pieces. Add carrots and potatoes into pot for the 2nd hour of cooking. Don't forget to put the lid back on.

After time is up, place biscuits all over the top of your stew and bake uncovered on 425 for about 8-10 minutes.

HINT: If you brown the meat before baking, the juices are sealed in better making the meat even juicier.

TIP: I like my carrots overcooked with no crunch, so I put them in for the entire 2 hours of cooking.

DESSERTS AND SWEETS
DOLCE

Homemade Pastry Dough
1 pie shell

1 1/3 cups flour
1/2 cup cold butter, cut into chunks
¼ tsp salt
2 tbsp sugar
2 tbsp water

You can do this in a food processor on pulse, but make sure not to over knead the dough or it will not be as tender, here is how:

In a food processor, put in all dry ingredients, then add butter a few pieces at a time, only using pulse option for each butter addition. Keep pulsing until the dough looks crumbly and comes away from the side. Give 2 or 3 more pulses and take out. Knead just to form the dough ball and place in a covered dish into the fridge for ½ hour to get cold again.

Cool dough in fridge for ½ hour, then take out and place on floured counter area, flour dough lightly and with a rolling pin or something long and round, roll out dough shaping a circle bigger than your pie pan. Fold in half and fold in quarter, then place the center point in middle of pie pan and open up, cut off excess, take a fork and dot a few holes around bottom. Bake 350 for 10 minutes. If this comes out puffy, take a fork and press fork side all across the bottom, flattening dough back out.

Double the recipes and here is what you can do with the top.

Take your second dough a repeat above only slice into ½ to 1 inch wide strips about 10 inch long. After criss-crossing on top, take a knife and run around outside of pie pan, trimming off all the excess dough. You can also egg wash at this point

HINT: Pastry dough is very forgiving, if you make a hole, patch it with the excess overhanging pie shell.

Apple Cake

Preheat oven to 350

2 beaten eggs
½ cup white sugar
½ cup brown sugar
1 cup flour
2 tsp baking powder
2 tsp vanilla
½ tsp salt
4 apples

Peel apples and dice into small pieces.

Mix all ingredients together, and then mix in apples

Pour into greased 9 inch pan, Bake 30 min

To make a vanilla glaze, take ½ cup confectionary sugar and add 2-4 tbsp warm water and 1 tsp vanilla. Add water 1 tbsp at a time. You are looking for the consistency of melted cheese. Pour this all over the top in thin lines back and forth

Apple Pie

Preheat oven to 325

7 large apples
1 ½ tbsp butter
1 tsp cinnamon
¾ cup sugar
1 tbsp flour
½ tsp salt
2 pie pastry

Pastry directions; see directions at the beginning of this section or go to grocery store, buy a ready made pie shell in the freezer section, and thaw out. Read directions on how to use but homemade is really simple to make.

Peel and slice apples, then mix all ingredients together except butter and pour into a pie pan with pastry. It will be mounded on top, now add little bits of butter all over top of pie. Take your second pie shell and after it is rolled out, cut slits all though out for air holes (to let out excess steam) Cover your pie and pinch all the way around sealing the two shells together. Take an egg and beat it then brush over top of pie.

Bake for 50 minutes

TIP; If you want to make sure you do not have a mess in the oven from dripping juices, place a flat sheet pan under the pie for baking.

HINT: Apples shrink down as they cook, use all your pie mix and over stuff your pie, it will become a better-filled pie.

Apple Strudel Cake

Preheat oven to 350

2 beaten eggs
¾ cup sugar
1 cup flour
2 tsp baking powder
2 tsp vanilla
½ tsp salt
½ tsp cinnamon
6 peeled and diced apples
¼ cup extra sugar and 1 tsp cinnamon for topping mix

Mix all ingredients, then add apples

Pour into greased 9 inch pan, mix topping and sprinkle all over top. Bake 30 min

Icing
½ cup confectionary sugar
2 tbsp water
1 tsp vanilla

Mix together and microwave for 30 seconds, mix again, then drizzle all over top of cake. Let cool.

> *Italian Proverb: If you scatter thorns, do not go barefoot.*
> *Meaning: Do no harm to others, it could come back to bite you.*

Boston Crème Pie

This is actually a cake with a custard center. My son Richard Jr. is a fan of custard filled anything. This is one of his favorites.

Preheat oven to 350

2 cups flour
1 ½ cups sugar
1 tbsp baking powder
¼ tsp salt
1/2 cup melted butter
1 cup milk
1 tsp vanilla
1 beaten egg

Cream butter and sugar, then mix in remaining ingredients until combined, mix egg in last. Put into 2 round buttered, floured pans. Bake for 30-40 minutes.

CUSTARD FILLING
1 cup milk
½ cup sugar
¼ cup corn starch
¼ tsp salt
2 beaten egg yolks
1 tsp vanilla

Meanwhile, do this next part stirring continually. In a pan on medium, heat milk, sugar, cornstarch and salt. Bring to a boil, then remove from heat, add ½ of this mix gradually to the egg yolks and beat together. This tempers the eggs to the heat. Return egg mix to saucepan, and on medium heat, bring to boil again. Remove from heat and whip in vanilla.

Make sure cake is cooled before putting crème on top of first cake, then place second cake on top and finish with the following..

In the microwave, melt 1 cup chocolate chips, 20 seconds at a time for close to 2 minutes. Slowly whip in ¼ cup milk. Dribble warm frosting on top of cake and let it drip down the sides.

Brownies

Preheat oven to 350

1 cup flour
1 cup sugar
½ cup melted butter
¼ cup cocoa powder
2 tbsp baking powder
¼ tsp salt
1 tsp vanilla
2 beaten eggs

Cream eggs, butter, vanilla & sugar, add remaining ingredients and blend. Pour into buttered and floured pan.

Bake 25 – 30 minutes depending on your oven but no longer.

HINT: They will be really soft when you take them out of the oven, giving the conclusion that they are not done enough. Trust me they will harden as they cool. If you overcook brownies, you end up with rocks.

TIP; Make this extra special and spread a chocolate gnache or even hot fudge on top.

> *The Italian Flag: Tricolore, has a green, white and red strip running side by side. The colors stand for Hope, Faith and Charity.*

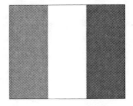

Chocolate Brownie Cake

Preheat oven to 375

2 ½ cups flour
2 tsp baking powder
3 ½ tbsp cocoa powder
½ tsp salt
1 ¼ cup sugar
1 cup milk
4 tbsp melted butter
2 tsp vanilla

Mix wet ingredients and dry ingredients separately. Then slowly mix the dry into wet.

Pour into a buttered and floured baking pan. Bake 35 minutes or until cake passes the fork test.

Options: Before baking sprinkle on top; nuts, chocolate chips or both.

> *The Sicilian Flag: Trinacria was an ancient name for Sicily and means triangle. It is meant to resemble the shape of Sicily. It is yellow and red, and has a woman's head with angel wings and with three bent legs that point to each cape in Sicily. It stands for good luck and prosperity.*

Chunky Brownies

Preheat oven to 325

1 ½ cups flour
½ tsp salt
1 cup sugar
1 cup brown sugar
3 eggs
½ cup melted butter
1 tbsp strong coffee or Kahlua
1 tsp vanilla
¼ cup milk
1 cup chocolate chips dipped in flour
1 cup walnuts dipped in flour

Mix eggs, butter, milk, vanilla and coffee. Add sugars and salt, and then add in flour. Make sure chips and nuts are coated in flour before adding them last.

Pour into a greased and floured baking pan and spread out on bottom. Bake 25 minutes. Take out and cool 20 minutes.

HINT: As brownies cool, they harden.

TIP: To make this a triple threat add a chocolate gnash on top

Chocolate Gnache
½ cup melted chocolate chips
¼ cup milk

Melt chip in the microwave for 20 seconds at a time, mixing in between each session. Stir in milk until completely blended.

Cannoli

This is one of my favorite desserts and most Italians too. You can buy ready made cannoli shells online or grocery store if you live in a big city.

SHELL
4 cups flour
1 egg yolk
1 tbsp sugar
¼ tsp salt
¼ tsp cinnamon
¼ cup red wine

Mix all shell ingredients together, roll out and cut 5 inch circles. Shape around metal cannoli tube and use egg wash or water to seal dough ends together on the form. Deep fry with the cannoli tube. After taking shell out of the oil, remove the tube while still warm. The shell is very pliable when warm. Let cool before stuffing.

CREAM FILLING
1 cup ricotta cheese
½ cup confectionary sugar
1 tbsp kahlua, Amaretto or strong coffee
½ tsp cinnamon
¼ cup chocolate chips (optional)

Blend all your crème ingredients together and put in fridge.

The easy thing to do if you do not have a pastry bag is put it in a baggy and snip the tip. This makes it easy to fill the shells without making a huge mess. After the cannolis are filled, sprinkle them with confectionary sugar all over the top.

TIP: Use ½ ricotta and ½ cream cheese to make a firmer crème. You can also use all crème cheese if you don't have Ricotta.

OPTIONAL: You can be creative, dip the ends of the shell before filling into melted chips and put in fridge to let harden. Also after filled you can dip the ends into chocolate chips or nuts.

Amaretto Cheesecake

This is my favorite cheesecake and so easy to make.

Preheat oven to 350

1 lb cream cheese
½ cup sugar
2 tbsp Amaretto or Almond Extract
2 eggs
1 graham cracker pie shell

Blend cheese, sugar, and Amaretto together, mix in beaten eggs. Pour into a graham cracker pie shell, put on water bath pan. Bake 50 minutes. It will rise high, and then settle back into itself after it starts to cool. Let cool overnight or at least 3 hours.

You can eat this plain or to give a little pizzazz or special occasions, make this for it:

Strawberry Sauce

1 cup strawberry
2 tsp Amaretto
1/8 cup sugar

Bring to boil and cook 10 minutes, then add

1 tsp water
1 tsp corn starch
Cook 2-3 minutes more and pour on top of cheesecake

Chocolate and Vanilla Cheesecake Pie

Preheat oven to 350

1 lb cream cheese softened
1 14 oz can condensed milk
¼ cup sugar
1 egg
¼ tsp salt
1 tbsp kahlua
1 tbsp flour
1 cup chocolate chips
1 graham cracker pie crust

In a food processor, mix together cheese, milk, sugar, salt, egg and kahlua until creamy.

In a baggy, put flour and chocolate chips and shake to coat all the chips. Add into cream cheese mix and then pour into pie crust.

Bake 40 minutes and let cool completely

TIP: A can of cherry pie mix makes a great and easy topping spooned on top of each slice before eating.

> *Sicilian Proverb: To he that watches, everything else is revealed.*
> *Meaning: Listen and learn*

Heavenly Chocolate Mousse Pie

This is an easy, no bake, no eggs mousse.

½ cup chocolate chips
½ cup condensed milk
1 tbsp Amaretto
2 cup heavy cream
½ cup sugar
¼ tsp salt
1 graham cracker pie crust
¼ cup shaved semi sweet chocolate bar

Melt your chips in the microwave on 20 second intervals, mixing as you melt. Mix in milk, salt and Amaretto.

Using a mixer, beat heavy cream and sugar into whipped cream. Divide into 2 sections and put ½ in the fridge for later.

Fold half of your whipped cream slowly, in sections into chocolate mix, pour into pie crust, and let cool. Spread remaining ½ of whipped cream and sprinkle shaved chocolate all over top.

> *Sicilian Proverb: Do not become a sheep unless you want to become a meal for a wolf.*
> *Meaning: Stand up for yourself and your beliefs. Sheep are easily led.*

Sementes Italian Cheese Cake

Catherine Semente was a long time friend of my grandmother. I remember her a little, but I remember hearing her name my whole life.

Preheat oven to 400

3 lbs Ricotta Cheese
8 eggs beaten
1 cup sugar
3 tbsp Amaretto
1 tsp vanilla extract

Mix all ingredients together well and pour into a greased round cake pan. Bake for 30 minutes on 400, then lower heat to 325 and bake for 60-70 minutes. Let cool at least 3 hours or overnight.

Pound Cake

Preheat oven to 325

1 cup flour
1 cup sugar
2 beaten eggs
½ cup melted butter
1 tsp vanilla or almond extract
Pinch of salt (1/8 tsp)

Sift, and then mix all ingredients together until combined, adding eggs in last. Spoon into a buttered and floured bread pan.

In a water bath, bake for 1 ¼ hours

HINT: Water bath is simply placing a pan of water in the oven to keep the air inside the oven moist.

Cinnamon Crumb Cake

Preheat oven to 350

2 ½ cups flour
1 cup sugar
3 beaten eggs
½ cup melted butter
¾ cup milk
1 tbsp baking powder
¼ tsp salt
1 tsp vanilla

Cream eggs, butter, vanilla & sugar, add in remaining ingredients and blend, but do not over mix. Pour into buttered and floured pan.

TOPPING
½ cup melted butter
¼ cup brown sugar
¼ cup sugar mixed
1 tsp cinnamon

Mix both sugars and cinnamon together.

Pour the melted butter over the cake as evenly as you can. Sprinkle sugar mix on top next.

Bake 30- 40 minutes depending on your oven.

Cranberry Orange Muffins

I discovered this muffin at one of my favorite restaurants with my friend Debbie, Sweet Tomatoes. I went home and immediately tried to duplicate the recipe. This is my version.

Preheat oven to 375

2 cups whole wheat or white flour
½ tsp salt
2 tsp baking powder
½ tsp baking soda
1 cup sugar
¼ cup safflower or canola oil
1 tsp almond extract or vanilla
1 egg
1 cup orange juice
½ cup minced cranberries
½ cup chopped nuts

Mix all ingredients together and pour into 12 cupcake tins. Bake for 20-25 minutes. Serve with butter spread on top.

Strawberry Marble Cake

Preheat oven to 325

1 cup flour
1 cup sugar
½ cup melted butter
¼ cup water
1 tsp vanilla or almond extract
Pinch of salt (1/8 tsp)
2 beaten eggs
¼ cup grenadine or cherry juice.

Sift flour, sugar and salt, then mix in butter, water, vanilla, then eggs last. Spoon more than ½ the batter into a buttered and floured bread pan. Add grenadine to remaining batter, mix then pour all over 1st batter, do not mix together. Bake 1 ¼ hours.

Stuffed Figs
Fichi

Since I have a fig tree in my backyard, I have an endless amount of figs in the summer now. To my surprise, my figs taste and eat like mini peaches when you eat them fresh, except, you can eat the whole fruit including the seeds.

Preheat oven to 400

24 Figs
1 cup chopped nuts
1 tbsp honey
1 tbsp amaretto
8 oz cream cheese

Clean and cut stalks off figs and slice an X into it half way down and put onto greased baking dish. Blend room temp cheese with all ingredients.

Place cheese into pastry bag with fairly large opening and fill each fig. Bake 15 minutes.

Grandma's Sponga Cake

Preheat oven to 350

4 eggs beaten
1 cup sugar
1 cup butter softened
2 tsp vanilla
3 ½ cups flour
2 tsp baking powder
½ tsp salt

Cream together sugar and butter. In a separate bowl mix flour, salt and baking powder. In another bowl beat eggs and add vanilla. Mix ingredients into creamed mix alternating floured and eggs until all combined. Pour into butter and flour pan and bake for 25 - 30 minutes, until golden brown and passes a fork test.

Fred's Holiday Fruitcake

Traditionally, Sicilian's do not include "fruitcake" in their holiday menus, they make fruit breads. I did not grow up eating fruitcake and was always afraid to try it. This one is an exception to the rule. My friend, Fred gave me this recipe. He makes this every Christmas and passes it around to his friends. This is surprisingly easy to do and really does taste great.

First bowl
3 sticks butter or 3/4 cup
1 lb marshmallows

Second Bowl
2 lbs candies cherries
1 lb candied pineapple
1 tsp cinnamon
1 box graham crackers

2 cups each chopped pecans, almonds, walnuts and brazil nuts.

In first bowl microwave butter, then microwave marshmallow and cream these two together.

Mix all ingredients of second bowl together well. Then add creamed mix in and mix like meatloaf. Takes muscle and I use my hands. Very messy.

Get 4 loaf pans and cover with large saran wrap enough to have a saran wrap lid. You can also buy small loaf pans and get more yield out of these

Pack mixture into loaf pans tightly and cover with remaining saran wrap. Put in fridge for 2 days to set up and cure.

TIP: I weigh these down by stacking on top of each other and adding a can of soda to weigh down the top loaf. In addition, during the next two days I rotate the pans to help with the packing down process.

Ice Cream Sandwiches
with Pizelle maker

If you have a Pizelle maker, this is really fun to make and the kids will love it.

2 eggs
1 cup sugar
¼ tsp salt
1 stick butter
2 cups flour
¼ cup cocoa powder
½ tsp vanilla

Mix all shell ingredients together, looks like cookie dough. Put 1 tbsp at a time on each pizelle plate and close for 30 seconds. Let cool completely.

Take 1 or 2 scoops of ice cream and put in center top it with another shell and press gently to get ice cream to side. Put in freezer immediately to reharden.

TIP: You can roll ice cream sandwich sides into chocolate chips, sprinkles, or chopped nuts.

HINT: If you don't have a Pizelle Maker, you can also bake them in the oven on 350 for 10 minutes. Make sure you leave room for spreading

Sicilian Honey Sweets
Struffoli

This cookie recipe from my Grandmother was a Christmas tradition that she made every year. She placed little silver sprinkle dots as a finishing touch all over her mountain of honey balls.

2 cups flour
6 eggs
¼ cup oil
½ cup water
½ cup sugar
½ tsp baking powder
½ tsp salt
1 tsp cinnamon
1 tsp vanilla or rum extract
8 oz candied fruit

Mix all ingredients together well. Work with your hands and turn into non-sticky dough. Add more flour if needed

Flour your working area. Cut dough into small workable pieces a little bigger than palm size. With your floured hands take a small piece and roll it with your hands until it looks like a long straw. Lay it down and repeat this until all dough has been rolled into straw shapes. If you lay all the straws next to each other, you will be able to cut a bunch at once. Now take a floured knife or spatula and chop the straws into ½ inch pieces. It helps to roll your floured hands lightly all over the dough balls to help form them better into the ball shape. You can also individually shape each cookie by hand if you want, remember they do not need to be perfect.

Heat a large frying pan of olive oil on medium. Fry all the cookie pieces, a little at a time until all are golden brown. Do not overcrowd your frying pan. Take out and drain off excess oil by placing them on paper towels.

Take your cookies and put them into a large bowl. Pour the honey mix into it, candied fruit, and gently mix to coat all of your cookie balls.

Get a platter and place all the cookies, making a cookie mountain on it. You can now decorate with sprinkles. Depending on the holiday, you can vary what type of sprinkle you use. For Christmas you can use red, green or silver. Easter can be multi-colored. In addition, you can even shape your cookie mountain into a wreath if you want.

Honey Mix

½ cup honey
3 tbsp sugar
3 tbsp water

Bring to a boil then simmer on medium until foam disappears and honey turns a clear yellow

TIP: ½ cup chopped candied cherries with your sprinkles also make a great decoration on this dish.

My Aunt Mary, who was the eldest child, would take everyone to the movies when they were all little. Back then it cost a nickel to get in and they would go on the special night each week, where they each received free promotional gifts from the theatre. She would make sure everyone was comfortable and as soon as the lights were dimmed, and the movie started, she would open her bag and take out the food she prepared for everyone as a snack during the show.

When my own kids were small, we would go to the movies every Tuesday because it was dollar day and I could afford for the kids to invite their friends. I also made little snack bags for everyone and made a stop at the store for candy and soda.

Camille and Vickie Muffins

Here is a recipe from my daughter and I messing around in the kitchen when she was little.

Preheat oven to 375

2 cups flour
¼ cup oil
½ cup melted butter
2 tsp baking powder
¼ cup cocoa powder
½ cup brown sugar
½ tsp salt
1 cup sugar
1 cup milk
2 tsp vanilla
½ cup chocolate chips

Mix wet ingredients and dry ingredients separately. Then slowly mix dry into wet.

Spoon into a buttered and floured muffin pan. Bake 35 minutes or until cake passes the fork test.

Ricotta Fritters

This is sort of an Italian hush puppy dessert.

2 cups self rising flour
2 cups Ricotta cheese
½ cup sugar
6 eggs
Powdered sugar for topping after frying

Mix all ingredients in a bowl except flour. Slowly mix in flour and beat until smooth. Drop into deep fryer by 1 tbsp at a time, turn after a few minutes, take out when golden on both sides and put on paper towels to drain excess oil and cool a couple of minutes, then sprinkle powdered sugar on top. These taste best warm.

Pumpkin Pie

Preheat oven to 400

I am calling this recipe a happy accident. I have never seen it cooked this way but I love the taste combination. I did this when I made too much pumpkin pie filling and it was more than the 1 pie shell I made could handle. I always have graham cracker shells around in case someone wants chocolate pie, so I used it.

2 - 12 oz cans pure pumpkin
½ cup heavy cream
½ cup milk
½ cup brown sugar
½ cup sugar
1 tsp nutmeg
1 tsp cinnamon
¼ tsp salt
3 eggs
1 large graham cracker pie shell

Heat pumpkin on medium, add all ingredients except eggs and mix well. Take off heat.

Beat eggs and slowly add some pumpkin pie mix into the eggs until you have added about a cup. This tempers the eggs so they become closer to the temperature of the pumpkin and tends not to scramble. Slowly add the egg mix back into the pumpkin mix.

Pour into pie shell and bake on 400 for 15 minutes, then lower to 350 and bake for 30 minutes. Let cool so it has a chance to set.

TIP: I put my pie onto a baking sheet just in case, so nothing spills onto oven floor.

Pecan Pie

Preheat oven to 325

4 beaten eggs
2/3 cup brown sugar
¾ cup corn syrup
3 tbsp melted butter
1 tsp vanilla
½ tsp salt
¼ tsp orange extract
1 ½ cup chopped pecans
1 cup pecan halves to use last.

Pastry directions;
With clean hands squeeze butter and flour together until all butter is incorporated into flour, should be very dry. Add 2 tbsp water, and if this is still too dry add another tbsp water.

Or in a food processor, add flour, butter, and pulse until incorporated, add 2 tbsp water and pulse, if needed add 1 last tbsp of water. Sometimes you do not need the extra water depending on the weather and humidity in the air. Put in fridge to cool 30 minutes.

When chilled, flour your hands, working area, and your pastry roller. Roll out your dough, then turn the dough 90 degrees and keep rolling until it is about 12 inched in diameter.

Take your pastry and fold in half then fold in half again into a triangle. Put in center of floured pie pan and unfold. You can now take a knife and score top edge to rid the excess or pinch under if not too much all around top. You can take a fork and press down to make a decorative top or do nothing else. Bake 10 min on 350.

Pie assembly directions;
Mix all ingredients together and pour into a pie pan with pastry.
Top with pecan halves starting on outer part of pie and completing a row circle, then put next row of pecans inside circle and do this until you have filled top with pecan halves. 0000000 like this.
                            0000000
Bake for 50 minutes

Ingredients for pie crust

1 1/3 cups flour
1/2 cup cold butter, cut into chunks
¼ tsp salt
2 tbsp sugar
2 tbsp water

Or go to grocery store and buy a ready made pie shell in the freezer section and thaw out. Read directions on how to use but it is easy to make your own.

Marble Pound Cake

Preheat oven to 325

½ cup melted butter
½ cup oil
2 ½ cups sugar
6 beaten eggs
2 tsp vanilla
¼ tsp salt
¼ tsp baking powder
3 cups flour
1/4 cup cocoa powder for later

Cream wet ingredients well.
In another bowl mix dry ingredients.
Slowly combine dry into wet. Mix until all blended

Pour about ¾ of the batter into a greased and floured 9 inch pan. Now add cocoa powder to remaining batter and mix well.

Slowly pour chocolate mix all over top of vanilla mix and do not mix them together. Bake 1 hour.

Stuffed Strawberries

This is my version of an old classic.

1 pint strawberries
8 oz crème cheese
½ cup sugar
2 tbsp Amaretto
2 or 3 graham cracker cookies

Blend room temp cheese, sugar, and Amaretto together. Place in fridge for 1-2 hours to chill back up.

Meanwhile prepare your strawberries. Clean, but leave the tops on and flip them onto their tops. Cut an X into the bottoms about half way down. Then gently spread apart each berry bottom, which will give you a large opening for the filling.

To make your graham cracker cookies, place cookies into a baggy and crush well. Place into a bowl. You can also crush these in a food processor.

Once your cheesecake filling is ready take a tbsp size and roll gently into graham crackers until all sides are coated. Do this until you run out of cheese. You can shape the cheese ball as you roll it. Put into fridge for 15 – 20 minutes to set back up again. Then take each cheese ball and place into opening of strawberries.

HINT: Hold the little green tops while eating this.

Vanilla Cake with Chocolate Gnache

Preheat oven to 375

1 cup sifted flour
½ cup sugar
½ cup butter
1 tsp baking powder
½ tsp salt
1 tsp vanilla
3 beaten eggs
¼ cup cold water

8 oz dark chocolate chips
¼ cup heavy cream
1 tsp vanilla extract

Cream eggs, vanilla, butter, sugar and water. Sift flour, salt, and baking powder. Slowly mix ingredients together. Pour into buttered and floured pan. Bake about 30 minutes depending on your oven.

Let cool, then remove from pan and place onto serving dish. Melt chips in the microwave and mix in vanilla and heavy cream, pour over top of cake, and spread all over.

TIP: This cake comes out real smooth if you sift the flour twice.

Sicilian Proverb: The habit does not change the monk. Meaning: Don't judge a book by its cover.

Vanilla Cake

Preheat oven to 350

3 cups flour
1 ½ cup sugar
2 tbsp baking powder
1 tsp salt
1 tsp vanilla
2 beaten eggs
1/3 cup melted butter
1 ½ cups milk

Cream together eggs, butter, vanilla, sugar and milk. Sift dry ingredients and add slowly into wet until combined. Pour into buttered and floured pan.

Bake 30- 40 minutes depending on your oven.

<u>Basic Icing</u>
1 lb box conf sugar
1 cup shortening or butter softened
1 tsp vanilla
½ tsp salt

Whip together 5 min

TIP: For chocolate icing, add ½ cup melted chocolate chips into whipped icing.

Italian Wheat Pie

This is another recipe that my Grandmother would make for special occasions and my Uncles remember her making it for them. This is an award winning dessert, and many Italians make this on Holidays.

Preheat oven to 375

2 lbs Ricotta Cheese
1 lb wheat
1 cup sugar
6 eggs beaten
1 tbsp oil
1 tbsp cinnamon
½ tsp salt
½ cup chocolate chips
8 oz mixed candies fruit minced (optional)
3 pie shells (store bought or homemade)
1 egg white for egg wash
confectionary sugar for topping later

In a pot, cook the wheat until tender on medium, about 30 minutes, drain out the excess water, add all remaining ingredients, and mix well. Pour into 2 pie shells.

Your last pie dough will cover both pies. Place strips of pie dough in a criss-cross on top of mixture. Take 1 egg white and add 1 tbsp water and mix to use for egg wash.

Bake 30-40 minutes until center is cooked and passes fork test. Let cool in the oven with the door slightly open. Sprinkle confectionary sugar on top after it has completely cooled.

TIP: If you can't find wheat to boil, you can use barley, but you don't need to preboil it.

Italian Fried Dough
Zeppole

This is a special treat for Italians to enjoy during St Josephs Day in March. My uncle Mino used to make this in the pizza place growing up, we would eat it warm right out of the fryer. This would compare to a funnel cake you find at the carnival.

1 package yeast (1 tbsp)
1 cup hot water
½ cup sugar
½ tsp salt
1 ½ cups flour
Powdered sugar for topping

In a pan mix water and yeast and let proof for 10 minutes. Mix in sugar, salt and flour and knead for 5 minutes until a satiny sheen comes over it, cover with a cloth or saran wrap and let sit for 1 ½ minutes to rise and double in size.

Take a handful at a time and drop into deep fryer but as you drop in, take your thumb and forefinger and cause a large hole in the middle of the dough, turn after a few minutes and take out when golden on both sides. Take out and put on paper towels to drain excess oil and cool a few of minutes, then sprinkle powdered sugar on top.

HINT: To let yeast proof, means letting it wake up. You will see bubbles form in the water as it does this.

TIP: You can put honey on top instead of sugar.

TIP: If you make these without causing a whole, you can cut these in half and fill with a little cannoli cheese..

COOKIES

AND

CANDIES
CARAMELLAS

Sicilian Fig Cookies
Cuccidata

This cookie recipe also came over from Sicily with my Grandma and was my favorite cookie that she made. You can vary on how to serve it, with or without filling, icing or sprinkles. I liked mine with just icing and no filling, but all ways are delicious.

Preheat oven to 375

First, mix until creamy:
1 cup melted butter
1 ½ cup sugar
1 tsp vanilla or rum extract
4 beaten eggs
½ tsp salt
½ tsp cinnamon

In a 2nd bowl mix;
4 ½ cups flour
4 ½ tsp baking powder

<u>Cuccidata with no filling</u>
Slowly mix dry ingredients into wet, add more flour if this does not turn into non sticky dough. When the dough does not stick to side or fingers, it is ready to work.

Flour working area. Cut dough into smaller pieces. With your floured hands take a baseball size or smaller piece and roll it until it looks like a long snake about 1 inch wide. Do this until all the dough is rolled. Next, take your hand and squish down so it is ½ inch high. Do this to the whole length of the cookie snake. Now take a knife or spatula, angle it and chop into 1 inch wide cookies that are diamond shaped. Place on baking sheet lined with parchment paper.

Bake for 15-20 minutes until turning golden

ICING/GLAZE
½ cup confectionary sugar
1 tsp vanilla
1-2 tbsp water
add 1 tbsp water at a time and more if needed.
Should be thick like warmed peanut butter

Take your cookie while it is still warm and dip top into icing mix. Lay onto a platter to cool and dry.

FIG FILLING
1 cup ground or minced calamyra figs
1 cup ground or minced dates
½ cup ground or finely chopped almonds
1 tbsp cinnamon
½ tsp salt
1 can mandarin orange crushed until pulpy, and keep juice
½ cup honey
3 tbsp Kahlua
3 tbsp Amaretto

Mix well and put into fridge to cure for at least 2 days before using.

<u>Filled Cuccidata</u>

Roll cookie dough until it is flat (like a pizza). Spread fig mix onto entire cookie except edges. Roll starting on one side the entire cookie like a cinnamon bun, and turn into a well fed snake. Slightly squish down entire snake, then take a knife or spatula and cut into 1 inch pieces. Take a fork and press it down on the sealed edges of cookie, both sides. Not the open fig sides. Put on cookie sheet and bake about 20 minutes or until golden. Dip warm cookie into icing or leave plain.

You can also add sprinkles after dipping for holidays.

TIP: I use my magic bullet to turn my figs into pulp. When doing this only mince a few figs at a time.

Easy Chocolate Fudge

1 ½ cups dark chocolate chips
1 can condensed milk
1 tsp vanilla
½ cup chopped hazelnuts

Melt all ingredients except nuts in a pan on medium heat and bring to boil while stirring occasionally. Reduce heat and cook 4 minutes on low. Take off heat and add in nuts. Pour into a pan lined with saran wrap. Cover with more saran and put into the refrigerator to cool.

Nutty Fudge

¾ cup melted butter
1/3 cup condensed milk
¼ cup sugar
12 oz dark chocolate chips
1 cup marshmallow cream
¼ tsp salt
½ cup chopped walnuts

Melt all ingredients except nuts in a pan on medium heat and bring to boil, reduce heat and cook 4 minutes on low. Take off heat and add nuts. Pour in a pan lined with saran wrap. Cover with more saran and put into refrigerator to cool.

Lady Fingers

These are very light cookies, used in Tiramisu, and other sweet desserts. I like to eat them with tea.

Preheat oven to 350

½ cup flour
¾ cup confectionary sugar
5 eggs separated - using both
½ tsp vanilla or Amaretto
¼ tsp salt

Beat egg whites into a meringue and add ¼ cup sugar

Mix ½ cup sugar with yolks, vanilla and flour. Fold in meringue mixture.

Fill a pastry bag and make small cigar shapes onto greased cookie sheet. Bake to golden 8 – 10 minutes.

HINT: Bring eggs to room temperature for better success with your meringue.

TIP: No pastry bag, use a large baggie and cut a ½ inch hole in a corner.

Italian Superstition: If you enter someone's house from one door, always leave the same way or bad luck can come your way.

Nutty Meringue Cookies

Preheat oven to 325

2 egg whites
½ cup confectionary sugar
1 tbsp vanilla
¼ cup chopped hazelnuts

Separate the eggs and let sit for 30 minutes so eggs can get to room temperature. Beat egg whites until stiff peaks form, then a little at a time add sugar, then add in vanilla. Fold in nuts, then spoon onto cookie sheet lined parchment paper. Bake 20 minutes.

TIP: Over a bowl, crack your egg in middle, then holding it upright, pull off top, the white should fall into bowl. Slowly transfer egg into empty shell top and this should get any remaining whites out leaving just the yolk in the shell. If you have pets, feed it to them or mix in their food, the yolk is great for their coat.

TIP: Use a mixer, do not use a magic bullet or blender, it did not work for me.

TIP: If you bring the eggs to room temperature, they will fluff better for you than if you try to beat them straight from the fridge.

Easy Almond Brittle

2 cups toasted and salted almonds
1 tsp butter
2 cups sugar
1 cup light corn syrup
½ cup water
1 tsp vanilla
1 tbsp baking soda

Cook almonds and butter for 10 minutes, then add sugar and water, cook for 10 minutes, then add vanilla and baking soda last, cook 10 minutes. Pour into a flat sheet pan and let cool. Then break into pieces.

Strawberry Cream Cheese Cookies

Preheat oven to 350

2 cups flour
1 box confectionary sugar
¼ tsp salt
1 cup butter softened
1 8 oz cream cheese
Strawberry jam

Mix ingredients and roll into a dough. Roll into tbsp size small balls then press down into center and flatten each cookie, with a tsp fill with a little jam, then bring up the sides and seal shut. Place onto greased cookie sheet. Bake about 15 minutes.

Sugar Cookies

Preheat oven to 325

2 ½ cups flour
1 ½ cups sugar
1 cup melted butter
1 tbsp baking powder
¼ tsp salt
2 tsp vanilla
1 beaten egg

Mix all ingredients together well. At this point, you have 2 choices.

You can take some wax paper, form a hotdog size roll out of the dough, and refrigerate for at least 1 hour. Then take out and slice ½ inch and place on your ungreased cookie sheet or you can spoon onto cookie sheet immediately and bake 8-10 minutes until your cookies just start turning golden.

Triple Chocolate Cookies

This is my best cookie and they do not usually last very long.

Preheat oven to 375

2 ½ cups flour
1 cup sugar
1 cup brown sugar
1 tsp baking powder
2 tsp vanilla
½ tsp salt
2 eggs
1 cup butter melted
¼ cup water
½ cup chocolate chips
½ cup chocolate chunks
½ cup mini M&Ms
½ cup walnuts (optional)

Mix wet ingredients and dry ingredients separately. Then slowly mix dry into wet. Drop tbsp size dough onto cookie sheet, give about 1 inch space. Cook about 12-14 minutes or until golden brown. If you like cookies chewier take out after 10 min, just as it starts to turn brown.

MISCELLANEOUS AND EMERGENCY COOKING RECIPES

Homemade Ricotta Cheese

This cheese is much tastier than what you buy in the store and so simple to make. You will be surprised at how much more flavor your homemade cheese has and it cost less to make than to buy.

9 cups milk
¼ cup lemon juice
1 tsp salt
Cheese cloth

In a large saucepan on medium heat milk until you see steam evaporating, add salt and lemon juice and slowly bring to a boil. Stir with a rubber spoon so milk does not scorch. Lower the heat a little and let simmer for about 5 more minutes. Keep stirring occasionally and scrape down sides. The liquid in the milk will turn yellow meaning the curds have all been made and what liquid is left is called whey, which you will drain off.

When you feel all the curds are made get a sifting colander and take your cheese cloth and fold into 4-6 levels, put it into the colander and pour cheese in and let drain. Then tie the cheese cloth to your faucet and let drain about 10-15 minutes. The longer you let it drain the drier it will be. Pour into a bowl and let it cool. At this point, it is almost a solid mass. Take a fork and slowly starting on one side, break up the cheese and fluff it out.

No preservative, so use within a week.

HINT: This cheese is drier than store bought so you will need to add a little water to some of your recipes to moisten the cheese.

TIP: If you like it creamier, drain less time about 5 minutes.

HINT: Do not squish down on it unless you want it really dry. You get about 2 cups or 1 lb of cheese from this.

TIP: No lemon juice, use white vinegar.

Yummy Peanut Butter Doggy Biscuits

Preheat oven to 325

1 cup uncooked oatmeal
1 cup corn meal
3 cups wheat flour
1 ½ cup hot water
2 beef bouillon cube
½ cup margarine melted
1 beaten egg
¼ cup peanut butter

Put bouillon cubes into hot water to melt. Mix all dry ingredients together, then add all wet into this, add peanut butter last. This becomes a fairly solid mass, if not, add a little more flour.

Roll out onto floured surface about ½ inch thick. Use a mini cookie cutter, cut into triangles or just cut into 1 inch strips, then cut strips into desired length depending on your dog's size. 1 inch for little, 2 for medium, 3 for large.

Put shapes on greased cookie sheet and cook about 60 minutes. You can put these pretty close together because they do not rise.

Allow them to cool completely and dry out into hard biscuits.

HINT: Some dogs have a wheat and corn allergy, this treat is not for them.

My grandpuppy, Pachino

HOMEMADE RECIPES

In case you have run out of these ingredients, here are some substitutions.

Condensed Milk

1/3 cup boiling water
¼ cup melted butter
1 cup sugar
1 tsp vanilla extract
1 cup powdered milk

Blend all liquid ingredients and add powdered milk last. Mix well.

Buttermilk

1 cup milk
1 tbsp vinegar or lemon juice.

Mix together and let sit for 5 minutes

Sour Cream

1/3 cup milk
1/3 cup melted butter

Heavy Cream (for cooking only)

1/3 cup melted butter
¾ cup milk

Meringue

2 egg whites
¼ cup sugar

Bring eggs to room temperature before beating

Chocolate Icing

8 oz chocolate chips
¾ cup heavy cream

Slowly heat cream to a gentle boil, then add few chips at a time until all melted, then turn into a bowl and stir 5 minutes until thick.

Vanilla Icing

3 cups confectionary sugar
½ cup soft butter or shortening
1 tsp vanilla

Beat for at least 5 minutes.

Vanilla Extract

12 vanilla beans
Vodka
Small dark bottle a little taller than the beans

After putting in beans fill to top with your favorite vodka, seal and let sit for about **1 month**.

Broth or Consume

1 bouillon cube
1 cup hot water

Basic Hollandaise Sauce

1 ½ sticks butter
4 large egg yolks
3 tbsp lemon juice
¼ tsp salt and pepper

Guacamole

2 mashed avocados
¼ cup chopped tomato without seeds
1 tsp onion and garlic powder
2 tbsp lime juice
½ tsp salt and pepper
1 tbsp mayo

Eggless Mayonnaise

¼ cup evaporated milk
2 tbsp white vinegar
¾ cup oil
¼ tsp white pepper
½ tsp salt
¼ tsp mustard

Mix together all ingredients except oil and vinegar. Slowly add in oil beating continually, now beat in vinegar. Done

Basic Gravy

2 cups water
2 bouillon cubes (beef or chicken)
2 tbsp flour
½ tsp salt and pepper

Melt bouillon into 1 cup hot water, then whisk flour into 1 cup cold water, add to hot and cook 2 minutes, salt and pepper last.

Baking Powder

½ tsp baking soda
½ tsp cream of tartar

Crock Pot Conversion Chart

Oven	High	Low
15 min	1 ½ hours	4 hours
30 min	3 hours	6 hours
45 min	4 hours	10 hours
3 hours	6 hours	18 hours

Approximate per pound Roasting Chart

Chicken	25 min
Pork	20-25 min
Beef Roast	25-30 min
Tenderloin	60 min
Fish	30 min
Ham	25 min
Turkey	15-20 min
Boston Butt	45 min
Lamb Roast	20 rare, 25 med, 30 well
Veal	40 min

Note: Cooking charts are with oven temp at 350°.

Basic Measurement Guide and Terms

3 tsp	= 1 tbsp
2 tbsp	= 1/8 cup
4 tbsp	= ¼ cup
8 tbsp	= ½ cup
12 tbsp	= ¾ cup
16 tbsp	= 1 cup = ½ pint
1 quart	= 2 pints + 4 cups
1 pkg yeast	= 1 tbsp
1 stick butter	= ½ cup = ¼ lb
16 oz	= 1 lb = 2 cups
8 egg white	= 1 cup
4 eggs	= 1 cup

1 tsp dry mustard = 1 tbsp prepared
1 cup rice makes 3 cups cooked
1 lb pasta makes 5 cups cooked
1 lb conf sugar = 3 ½ cups
1 tbsp fresh herbs = 1 tsp dried
1 tbsp cornstarch = 2 tbsp flour

1 tbsp	= Sprinkling, which is to cover top of dish with a layer of seasoning.
Al dente	= Having a little chew or bite to it, not completely cooked but almost.
Fork Test	= Insert fork or toothpick and it should come out clean.
Foil Tent/Hat	= Taking 2 long rectangle pieces of foil and combining to form a large square.
Snake shape	= Rolling dough into a long 1 inch wide tube
Straw shape	= Rolling dough into a long ½ wide tube
Well	= taking a pile of flour and making the center empty like a doughnut
Cream	= blending very thoroughly until creamy
Water Bath	= putting a pan of water in the oven while baking

INDEX

Almond Brittle, Easy, 140
Artichoke Dip, 11
Artichoke, Steamed, 10
Asparagus, Easy Cheesy, 56
Bagels, Cinnamon, 37
Baked Beans, Delicious, 56
Banana Bread, Yogurt, 26
Banana Nut Bread, 26
Biscuits, Buttermilk, 27
Bread, Carol's Irish Soda, 35
Bread, Cranberry, 31
Bread, Focaccia, 14
Bread, Garlic, 14
Bread, Pumpkin, 31
Bread, Queen Victoria's Cranberry Scone, 35
Bread, Tuscan Sweet, 36
Broccoli and Cheese Hamburger Macaroni, 71
Broth or Consume, 147
Brownies, 111
Brownies, Chunky, 113
Buttermilk, 146
Cabbage & Sausage, Italian, 77
Cabbage, Stuffed, 78
Cake, Apple, 107
Cake, Apple Strudel, 109
Cake, Chocolate Brownie, 112
Cake, Cinnamon Crumb, 119
Cake, Grandma's Sponga, 121
Cake, Marble Pound, 129
Cake, Pound, 118
Cake, Sementes Italian Cheese, 118
Cake, Strawberry Marble, 120
Cake, Vanilla with Chocolate Gnache, 131
Cannoli, 114
Casserole, Annie's Sweet Potato, 63
Casserole, Cowboy, 84
Casserole, Melissa's Famous Tater Tot, 99
Casserole, Pineapple, 62
Cauliflower, Sicilian Fried, 57
Cheese, Fried Mozzarella Sticks, 17
Cheesecake, Amaretto, 115
Chicken and Rice Alfredo, 73
Chicken Cacciatore, 81
Chicken Kabobs, Grilled Asian, 79

Chicken Lo Mein, Salvation, 82
Chicken Scaloppini, Stuffed, 74
Chicken Thighs, Crispy Baked, 80
Chicken Whoppers, 83
Chicken Wings, Party, 70
Chili, Quick and Easy, 79
Chocolate Gnache, 113
Clam Chowder, New England, 42
Condensed Milk, 146
Cookie, Sicilian Fig Cuccidata, 136
Cookies, Nutty Meringue, 140
Cookies, Strawberry Cream Cheese, 141
Cookies, Sugar, 141
Cookies, Triple Chocolate, 142
Corn Casserole, Cheesy, 58
Corn Casserole, Company, 58
Cornbread, Honey, 28
Cornbread, Original, 28
Crock Pot Conversion, 149
Cucumber Canape, Italian Herbed, 11
Dip, Fiesta Cheddar, 15
Doggy Biscuits, Yummy Peanut Butter, 145
Dressing, Honey Orange, 54
Dressing, Sweet Italian Salad, 54
Egg In A Hole, 17
Egg Rolls Lumpia, 60
Eggplant Parmesan, 88
Eggplant, Caponata, 13
Eggs, Deviled, 12
Figs, Stuffed Fichi, 121
Fried Dough, Italian Zeppole, 134
Fudge, Easy Chocolate, 138
Fudge, Nutty, 138
Fuitcake, Fred's Holiday, 122
Gravy, Basic, 148
Gravy, Sausage, 65
Guacamole, 148
Hamburgers, Grilled Mushroom, 94
Heavy Cream, 146
Hollandaise Sauce, 147
Hotdogs, Pigs in a Blanket, 15
Ice Cream Sandwiches, 123
Iced Tea, Sweet, 21
Icing, Chocolate, 147
Icing, Vanilla, 147
Italian Bread, Homemade, 29
Italian Easter Baskets Easter Bread, 30
Lady Fingers, 139

Lasagna, Baked, 90
Lasagna, Carol's Sausage and Mushroom, 72
Lemonade, 21
Linguine Noodles, Homemade, 59
Manicotti, 85
Mayonaise, Eggless, 148
Measurement Guide, 150
Meatballs, Matthew's Sweet and Sour, 92
Meatloaf, Italian Style, 93
Meringue, 146
Muffins, Camille and Vickie, 126
Muffins, Cranberry Orange, 120
Mushrooms, Stuffed, 16
Pancakes, Blueberry Ricotta, 33
Pancakes, Plain, 32
Pancakes, Potato, 34
Pastry Dough, Homemade, 106
Peppers, Camille's Stuffed, 95
Pie, Apple, 108
Pie, Boston Crème, 110
Pie, Chocolate and Vanilla Cheesecake, 116
Pie, Heavenly Chocolate Mousse, 117
Pie, Italian Wheat, 133
Pie, Pecan, 128
Pie, Pumpkin, 127

Pizza Bread, 18
Pork Chops, Carol's Italian Style, 82
Potatoes, Grandma's Italian Roasted, 64
Potatoes, Lumpy Mashed, 61
Potatoes, Scalloped, 66
Punch, Cranberry Party, 22
Punch, Fruity Party, 22
Punch, Pretty Party, 23
Quesadillas, Cheesy, 19
Ricotta Cheese, Homemade, 144
Ricotta Fritters, 126
Roasting Chart, 149
Salad, Charlene's Broccoli, 57
Salad, Dinner Fruit, 49
Salad, Garden Pasta, 52
Salad, Italian Style Potato, 53
Salad, Macaroni, 50
Salad, Matthew's Party Pasta, 51
Salmon Patties, 97
Sangria, Fruity, 23
Sausage Eggplant Parmesan, Mike's, 86
Shrimp Cocktail, Party, 20
Shrimp Fra Diavolo, 98
Shrimp Marsala, 98
Soup, Charlene's Easy Onion, 45
Soup, Chicken Noodle, 41

Soup, Fat Burning Cabbage, 40
Soup, Italian Sausage, 47
Soup, Minestrone, 44
Soup, Sandy's Vegetable Beef, 48
Soup, Sicilian Meatball, 43
Soup, Split Pea, 46
Sour Cream, 146
Spaghetti and Meatballs, 100
Stew, Corned Beef and Cabbage, 76
Stew, Italian Poor Man, 96
Stew, Lori's Western, 104
Stew, Oyster, 45
Strawberries, Stuffed, 130
Strawberry Sauce, 115
Tarter Sauce, Quick, 97
Tomato Juice, Almost V-8 Spicy, 23
Tomatoes, Summer Stuffed, 19
Turkey with Italian Style Stuffing, 102
Vanilla Extract, 147
Yorkshire Pudding, Charlene's, 27
Ziti, Baked Vickie's ABZD, 68
Zucchini Agridolci, 65

The family Coat of Arms